So You Want
To Be A Doctor?

C000261510

Official
Know-It-All
Guide™

Niriksha Malladi, M.D.

Frederick Fell Publishers, Inc.
2131 Hollywood Boulevard, Suite 305
Hollywood, Florida 33020
954-925-5242
e-mail: fellpub@aol.com
Visit our Web site at www.fellpub.com

This publication is designed to provide accurate and authoritative information in regard to the subject matter covered. *This book is not intended to replace the advice and guidance of a trained physician nor is it intended to encourage self-treatment of illness or medical disease. Although the case his-tories presented are true, all names of patients have been changed.*

Library of Congress Cataloging-in-Publication Data

Malladi, MD, Nirikisha, -
  So You Want To Become A Doctor? Fell's KIA/ by Dr. Nirikisha Malladi.
      p. cm.
  ISBN 0-88391-135-3 (trade pbk. : alk. paper)
  1. Self-Help. I. Medical.
  GV995.R55 2005
  796.342--dc22

                              2005010875

Interior and Cover Design- Chris Hetzer, IATPI

TABLE OF CONTENTS

Dedication:

To Anil and Mayuri, for being my inspiration. Everyone should be as fortunate as me. To Amma and Taji, for your unwavering support and gentle guidance. To Dr. Sandhu, your passion for medicine left an impression from the very beginning.

Acknowledgements:

This doctor's education wouldn't have been possible without the guidance of all my mentors. My gratitude to Dr. Ken Bryant, Ali van Klei, Deanna Reder, Karen Saenger, Dr. Stephen van Eeden, Dr. Rao, Dr. Rusnak, Dr. Gill and the countless patients who allowed me to learn by their bedside.

My thanks to Dr. Andrew Seal for allowing the use of his graduation address, and to salary.com for sharing information on physician compensation.

Reprint permission for *Perceptions of Medical School Deans and State Medical Society Executives About Physician Supply* by Dr. Richard Cooper, Medical College of Wisconsin Health Policy Institute. Original article published in Journal of American Medical Association, Dec. 10, 2003, Vol. 290, No. 22.

Reprint permission for information on the Canadian Residency Match by the Canadian Residency Matching Service.

Names of patients and physicians have been changed in the book to protect their privacy, although I wish I could mention them all to show my gratitude for their teachings.

Introduction:

So You Want to Be a Doctor? is a book for anyone looking for definitive information on how to become a doctor. Written by a medical school graduate, the book offers proven strategies to guide you through the formative pre-medical years. It covers all the qualifications sought by Medical School Admissions Committees, and provides insider guidance for high school and college students for admission into medical school.

Unique features of the book include:

Fool-proof strategies for becoming a strong medical school candidate

Advice on obtaining outstanding letters of recommendation

Sample answers as a guide to the medical school interview questions

Dedicated sections for minorities and older students on choosing the right educational programs

Options for a dual degree in medical school

Advice on getting a free medical education through national programs

Alternatives to traditional medical education, such as osteopathic medical school and foreign medical schools

Information on obtaining a Canadian medical education

Accounts of life on the hospital wards for a medical trainee

More than just being a how-to book for getting into medical school, it goes a step further to show you what to expect as you go through the medical curriculum, and internship. It illustrates the realities of medical education through anecdotes and real-life experiences of a doctor-in-training. Those seeking information on specialty training will find topics that aren't discussed during medical school, such as choosing the right field by considering lifestyle, compensation, and areas of need.

It is now more important than ever to look at the field of medicine in its entirety before deciding to enter it. Physicians joining the profession today face pressures as never before – such as soaring educational debt and a highly litigious environment. Yet, being a medical professional is synonymous with providing hope. Medicine will continue to be a beacon for anyone with a desire to help. This book will let you weigh the benefits of the profession against its challenges to arrive at an informed career decision.

The decision about the path of your life should be based on practicality as well as passion. There is no denying that the road to becoming a doctor is long and arduous, but anything worth doing will have its challenges. When I started medical school, I had vague notions about the many advantages that a career in medicine offered: intellectual stimulation, independence, prestige, financial stability, and the opportunity to make a meaningful contribution. What I hadn't realized was that the biggest reward came without such a ready label. Dr. Andrew Seal, Surgeon and former Associate Dean of Student Affairs at my alma mater, captured its essence in his graduation address to my class when he spoke about what it means to listen to patients: *"We listen to the sounds of their hearts, lubdub lubdub, the depths of their lungs, the sounds of peristalsis and occasionally borborygmi, if only we knew how to spell it; but most of all we listen to their stories. Over the years I have learned so much from my patients, listening to their stories, and have found my most rewarding moments to have been those when I have made time to sit quietly with them, alone, unhurried, perhaps at the end of the day, hearing of their lives, their families, their hopes and fears. You know, the greatest rewards you will have will be those that no one else will know about; they will be personal and private, and you will treasure them."*

Choosing the right career is one of the most important decisions you will have to make. If you think medicine may be the right profession for you, then just learning about how to get into medical school is not enough. This book will take you through the entire spectrum – from submitting your medical school applications to working as an MD

As Goethe put it *'One can be instructed in society, one is inspired only in solitude'*. Here's to finding your calling through reading and reflection.

- Niriksha Malladi, MD

How This Book Is Organized

Part 1 focuses on getting into medical school. It is divided into 6 chapters. In Chapter 1, we'll take a look at the present employment prospects for doctors and the odds of getting into medical school. If you're contemplating choosing medicine as a career, this chapter will elucidate what makes a good doctor. It will help you answer the question of why you may want to pursue medicine, and it will tell you about the different types of candidates being accepted into medical school all over the country.

Chapter 2 is for high school students who are considering going to medical school. It provides all the paths to becoming a doctor, either directly from high school or after obtaining an undergraduate degree. High school students will learn strategies for planning ahead to greatly increase their chances of medical school acceptance. They will learn the importance of becoming a diverse candidate, and are given tips for choosing an undergraduate degree.

In Chapter 3, undergraduate students in college and university will find the short track to becoming a strong medical school candidate. The CARE mantra is a mnemonic for the criteria sought by medical schools, and students will learn how to use it to their maximum advantage. Strategies for planning ahead in college and the best time to apply to medical school will be discussed.

Chapter 4 takes us into the application process for medical school, and finding the means to pay for the expensive education. You'll find sections on which medical schools will want you based on your unique qualifications, as well as the criteria by which you should evaluate medical schools. The process of organizing yourself through the college years is greatly simplified in the 'Suggested Timeline for the Application Process' at the end of the chapter.

Chapter 5 covers the most important parts of the application – letters of recommendation, personal statement and the Medical College Admissions Test. No part of the application should be approached without thorough preparation. This chapter gives the precise information needed to obtain outstanding letters of recommendation, and write a winning personal statement. The components of the Medical College Admissions Test are described.

And because acceptance won't be granted without a personal meeting with the members of the Admissions Committee, Chapter 6 provides a thorough preparation for the medical school interview. It gives details on common interview themes, and provides an opportunity for practice with sample interview questions and answers. You will also get tips on the types of questions you need to ask the Admissions Committee.

Part 2 is comprised of Chapters 7 and 8. It focuses on groups of students who deserve special mention.

Chapter 7 is for minorities and economically disadvantaged students, military students (or those interested in a medical/military career and a free education), and older students. In addition, students who want to enter a dual degree program will learn how to get a law degree, PhD, and Masters in Business or Public Health while completing a Doctor of Medicine degree.

Chapter 8 gives the closest alternative to an MD degree in the United States – an Osteopathic Medical degree. This chapter covers the basics on Osteopathic Medicine, medical school curriculum, the costs, and the advantages and disadvantages of such an option.

Part 3 discusses the option of pursuing a medical education outside of the U.S., in Canada as well as other countries. It consists of Chapters 9 and 10.

Chapter 9 addresses the key questions and doubts that students may have about learning medicine in a foreign country. It gives advice on choosing pro-grams that will ensure a quality education and allow you to return to practice med-icine in North America.

In Chapter 10, anyone considering going to medical school in Canada will find that the criteria for admission is identical to that in the U.S. The differences arise during post-graduate training. The chapter covers the basics on the key dif-ferences, and how to obtain a Canadian residency position.

Part 4 is a must-read for finding out what medical school is like during the four years of training It consists of Chapters 11 and 12.

Chapter 11 goes through my own training to provide an insider's glimpse into the first two years of medical school. It describes the curriculum, and tells you what to expect as you start your transformation from student to doctor.

Chapter 12 gives an overview of the clinical rotations, and gives a glimpse into the experiences of working in a hospital for the first time. It takes you into the moments shared with patients that become the cornerstone of a doctor's training.

Sections on elective rotations and my experience with an international elective provide a look at the exciting opportunities present within medical training.

Part 4 is comprised of Chapters 13 and 14. It focuses on the years following medical school.

Chapter 13 shows what is required of graduating students. It covers how students match to a residency of their choice, what hours they can expect to work, and what type of life they will lead before qualifying as an independent medical practitioner. It details a typical day in the life of an intern on call.

Chapter 14 discusses the topics that nobody will tell you in medical school. What are the most needed specialties? Which geographical areas require doctors? What are the possible career choices for an MD? What are income levels for different specialties? You will learn the key issues to consider before deciding on a career choice.

Finally, the appendices supplement the chapters. Appendix A gives a listing of the programs offering combined medical and undergraduate degrees. Appendix B provides a list of popular foreign medical schools attended by American and Canadian students. Appendix C gives a listing of Canadian medical schools.

Part 1: Getting into Medical School

Introduction to Part One:

If you've been thinking about applying to medical school, this part provides the map on how to become a successful applicant. It starts by looking at the qualities that make a good doctor and the duties of a physician in today's society. Then, it discusses the academic and non-academic criteria sought by medical schools. High school and undergraduate students are given the proven strategies for becoming strong candidates and excelling at the medical school admissions process. What is the best time to apply? Which schools will rank you highly? Is it affordable? All these questions are answered, with attention on giving you the best possible advantage. It details the secrets to obtaining strong letters of recommendation, to the best way of answering the tough medical school interview questions. There is a right and wrong way of approaching medical school. The following chapters will help you forge out your path.

Chapter 1: Is Medicine the Right Decision for You?

My mother said to me, "If you become a soldier, you'll be a general. If you become a monk, you'll end up as the Pope." Instead, I became a painter, and wound up as Picasso.
                    - Pablo Picasso

Finding our true calling may be the hardest responsibility thrust onto us early in life. Grade school allows us to ignore thinking about it, as we don't have the maturity to decide yet. High school asks the question gently, but tries not to unbalance our temperaments too much. Our volatile hormones might rebel at the thought of responsibility. Even the first part of college allows us to deny its existence. But sooner or later, that nagging thought reaches out, grabs at your jugular, and now it's furious. What will you do with the rest of your life?
Good question.

- Are you looking for a career that is stimulating, flexible, emotionally gratifying, honorable and financially rewarding?
- Are you interested in the human body, with all its intricacies and potential for disease?
- Do you have the potential to think like a scientist and comfort a sick patient at the same time?
- Do you take interest in communicating knowledge to others?
- Are you committed to making a difference in people's lives?

If you find yourself motivated by these questions, have you ever considered becoming a doctor?
Making a decision about your career can be harrowing, whether it's your first occupation or a change in your vocation. With the thousands of possibilities that today's job market presents, we are supposed to choose the single one that will satisfy all our needs. That's a formidable task for anyone. But if, deep inside, you've ever imagined yourself as a skilled surgeon performing a life-saving sur-

gery, or an eye doctor restoring sight to a child, allow the thought that this is truly possible. And the best part is that medical training makes these wonders possible every day. If you have ever dreamt of becoming a doctor, isn't it worth that dream to find out whether or not it is right for you?

Different fields of medicine are developing as we become more innovative and technologically sophisticated in our ability to fight disease. New specialties and sub-specialties will continue to evolve as our knowledge advances. Whether you are seeking to be the typical white coat doctor figure etched in our minds, or a researcher who uses medical knowledge to advance the frontiers of medicine, there is tremendous scope within the medical field to build a career according to your interests.

Choosing a profession in medicine is a life-altering decision. It requires careful consideration of the long years of study and personal sacrifices that will be demanded of you. It isn't a job that you can walk away from at the end of the day. It'll track you down everywhere - in the parking lot, at the grocery store, on your vacation. (Does anyone know who invented the pager so I can send him a personal letter of thanks?) It demands complete devotion during the training years, and will not accept the need for sleep, food or rest if a life is at stake.

And yet, the field of medicine continues to draw some of the brightest minds each year. All for the simple reason that there is no other profession like it. It is by striving to help others that you will discover life's true call within you. You will be humbled by the trust patients will place in your capable hands. As a fledgling medical student, you will promise yourself to never forget each special moment that comes your way. The first delivery, the first patient who proudly introduces you to her family as 'my doctor', the first life you save from an untimely death. Imagine an existence built on these moments, and you will understand why many practicing doctors consider the struggles to be worth it.

However, as in any other field, you should not be expected to make an invested career choice without the benefit of compelling labor market information for guidance in the decision making process. Let's look at some facts and figures.

Employment prospects

According to the U.S. Department of Labor, the healthcare industry is one of the two fastest growing fields for careers. The prospects within this discipline are abundant.

The nursing profession has struggled with a critical shortage in the U.S. and Canada for the past decade. The demand for pharmacists, physical therapists, physician assistants, healthcare technicians and hospital support staff continues to grow as our aging population faces increased medical needs. Doctors are pivotal in this growth, as they provide leadership to the rest of the healthcare team when it comes to patient care.

There are presently 780,000 physicians practicing in the United States today. Is there room to absorb more? The answer is an emphatic yes. In 2004, physician groups and governmental licensing bodies both expressed concerns regarding upcoming physician shortages in the United States. Certain areas of the country and specialties are expected to feel a greater impact of the shortfall than others, and the specifics of these issues are presently under study at the Center for Health Workforce Studies, State University of New York. To prevent the imminent predicted shortfall, the government-appointed Council for Graduate Medical Education has recommended a fifteen percent increase in medical student seats by 2015. There is an estimated demand for 300,000 more physicians over the next twenty years to maintain adequate access to medical care.

The reasons for the undersupply of doctors can be traced to two main factors: a fixed number of medical graduates per year despite a rapidly increasing population, and doctors choosing to maintain a life outside work and working less hours. Stricter work visa requirements will also affect the availability of foreign medical graduates, who currently comprise 25% of the physician work force. The increased need for medical graduates is already being felt in hospital residency programs across the country.

The flip side to assessing demand is looking at the supply of medical school candidates. Let's consider some of the numbers involved in the medical schools admissions process.

In the 1990's, application to medical school was at an all-time high when approximately 47,000 applicants competed for 17,000 medical student seats. The competition was ruthless, and increased numbers of American students left for foreign shores to get medical degrees. Following 1996, a substantial decline occurred in the number of interested applicants. The strong economy and stock market boom at that time made the business and information technology markets a more attractive option. The downward trend has persisted, and presently, the number of applicants stands around 35,000. So how does this benefit you?

The figures show that the odds of being accepted are presently 1 in 2. If you are still in the contemplation phase of applying for medical school, you couldn't have chosen a better time.

Favorable labor market conditions have their own value when assessing future prospects, but it is worth stressing at this point that becoming a doctor is not only a career, it is a privilege. **It will allow you to put a finger on the pulse of humanity, and feel its heart beating. Souls will be bared in your presence.**

Your eyes and heart will bear witness to many births and deaths. And it will always remain a privilege.

The Illustrious Halls of Medicine

By entering into the halls of medicine, you will be joining the ranks of physicians before you who made an indelible mark on this world. Our society has been fortunate to have had the great scientific minds of Harvey, Jenner, Withering and Banting, among countless other physicians. Without them, we wouldn't have seen great advances in the fields of physiology and immunology, and medical therapies such as digitalis and insulin. Even medical students have made historic contributions, such as Laennec, Freud and Best.

Medicine is a rare field that allows expression of service to humanity in many forms. Physicians have not limited their contributions solely within a scientific scope either. One only needs to look at some of the outstanding writers of our time to find the interwoven beauty of the science and art of medicine in their works: Dr. Somerset Maugham, Dr. William Carlos Williams, Dr. Arthur Conan Doyle, Dr. Oliver Wendell Holmes and Dr. Anton Chekov, to name just a few.

From the Past to the Present

Advances in medicine have been a collaborative effort from the days of Hippocrates 2400 years ago. From gaining knowledge of human anatomy to pharmacology, we now understand the effects of the environment on our physical health. The past seven decades in particular, has seen the downward spiral of diseases such as cholera and malaria, and even eradication of smallpox in 1979. In 1900, the three leading causes of death were pneumonia, tuberculosis, and diarrhea. Today, these infectious diseases are easily treatable. Instead, we are battling with chronic conditions such as heart disease, cancer and stroke as the leading killers. The average life span in 1900 was 49 years of age. In the year 2000, it had jumped to 77 years. This has been a tremendous accomplishment, and is also partially responsible for bringing chronic conditions to the forefront, as these diseases tend to show their presence with advanced age.

A field such as medicine that has had such an impact on human mortality couldn't have escaped following an often jagged path down the roads of history, however. While medicine has been present as far back as man has lived, as evidenced by etchings made of healers on cave walls thousands of years ago, the present realities of medicine are relatively new. It has taken an enormous span of time to fill in the gaps in knowledge, and challenges still remain.

It seems incredible to consider now that textbooks of medicine published in the 1930s made no recommendations for treatment of bacterial diseases. It wasn't until 1940 that penicillin was tried for the first time on a human. It was used in England on a policeman with bacterial blood poisoning. The patient did well while the medication was being given, but once the limited supply of penicillin ran out, he succumbed to the disease. Penicillin treatment was only attempted again once sufficient supply was available. The second patient survived, and the field of antimicrobials has never looked back. Dr. Fleming was awarded the Nobel Prize for his discovery in 1945. He is noted to have remarked: "Everywhere I go people want to thank me for saving their lives. I really don't know why they do that. Nature created penicillin. I only found it."

A Physician's Duty Does Not Change

Our present medical knowledge is again at the brinks of a revolution with emerging information on genetic encoding and treatments. Textbooks in use today might seem devoid of knowledge to future generations of medical scientists, but the basic value of the physician will remain unchanged. Becoming a better physician with each patient encounter will always remain the goal of both the young and the experienced medical doctor. **The work of a doctor lies in balancing medicine's scientific applications with the human needs that all patients have - the desire to be understood, reassured and helped. Our patients are our teachers, and we can only begin to understand their experiences by placing their diseases in context of who they are.** Their spiritual, intellectual, emotional, social and physical environment all contribute in some manner to their illness and recovery. It is the physician's duty to comprehend it all, and embark on the intriguing quest of utilizing all modes of recovery to provide relief. The words of Hippocrates, the Father and Founder of Medicine, will remind and guide us: "Where there is love of humanity, there is love of the art of medicine."

The Makings of a Good Doctor

I once heard an elderly female patient comment: "He's such a good doctor. I recommend him to everybody". She was referring to my Family Practice Attending Physician. I was a medical student in his clinic at that time, and the only difference that I had noticed that set him apart from his colleagues was that he greeted each patient warmly by shaking their hand and smiling into their eyes, even if it was their fifth visit to see him that month. I asked the patient what she liked about him. "Well, he's such a gentleman," she replied. That was my first lesson in bedside manner.

Hippocrates once said: "Some patients, though conscious that their condition is perilous, recover their health simply through their contentment with the goodness of the physician." There has been much criticism of the increasing lack of humane care in modern medicine today. Technical expertise has likely played a role in patients being seen as human bodies with diseases rather than as individuals with often painful illnesses. Gaining back our patient's trust therefore becomes one of the highest duties of a medical doctor entering training today.

The importance of communicating well with patients has found an important place in medical school curriculums in the western world. Patients rely on all physicians to have sound clinical judgment, and a medical school degree is seen as evidence of possessing all the skills necessary to diagnose and treat them effectively. Since patients cannot judge physicians by quizzing them on the basic mechanisms of disease, or the latest in evidence based medicine, they look for other familiar criteria to evaluate. Qualities such as empathy, good listening skills, caring and personal attention rank high consistently in patient studies. **Interestingly, physicians who were determined to have good communication skills also had a significantly lower rate of malpractice lawsuits.**

A good doctor will wear many hats and do it with grace. It is not one who accurately diagnoses at the first onset of disease, as illnesses can be like chameleons, and not reveal themselves until their distinctive shapes become visible. It is not one who can make the best predictions for cure rates, as each patient is an individual and not a statistic. It is not one who appears to know everything about diseases, as our ignorance in many areas is still glaring and half of our knowledge base is replaced every few years with more current information. A good doctor will, however, aid in his patient's recovery by being honest, approachable, wise in his advice, optimistic, dedicated to lifelong learning, balanced, a clear thinker, an inquisitive scientist, knowledgeable and kind. He will strive to understand instead of moralize, to lead gently but firmly towards healthier lifestyle choices, to educate clearly and be open to learning themselves. These are the hallmarks of a good doctor.

Why Do You Want to Be a Doctor?

Whether or not medicine is the right decision for you is a question that must be personally asked and answered. 'Why do you want to be a doctor?' will be asked at every medical school interview, and needs to be responded to without any hesitation or doubt. It is on the basis of your response that your commitment to the profession will be initially judged.

Many candidates are drawn to the field out of a desire to help the sick and wounded. It may invoke the altruistic nature inherent in us. Some may have been patients themselves in the past, and learnt enough medicine in the process, or seen sufficient deficiencies that they feel they can be of help to others. A large percentage of medical students are the children of physicians, and have been in training all their lives to enter medical school - either through parental encouragement or their own desire to be of service to others. Some might have been fortunate to have had powerful physician role models in their lives, and choose to emulate themselves after them. Still others are drawn for the respect and lifestyle that a physician's life offers.

None of these answers is wrong. Some may have more appeal from the perspective of the medical school Dean of Admissions, but on a personal level, all are powerful motivators. Choosing medicine solely for lifestyle, however, must be cautioned. Medicine is no longer as lucrative as it had once been, and while doctors still rank high in earnings, there are other professions such as business and information technology that require less in terms of time commitment and personal sacrifices. **Most importantly, pursuing medicine solely for financial rewards will leave you unfulfilled and resentful.**

Similarly, choosing medicine because dad and granddad were also physicians is not advised. While you may have a good grasp of the dedication and time commitment required by the profession, you will be more prone to experiencing stress and burnout at an early stage unless there is a deeper motivation for pursuing medicine. Many physicians agree that the practice of medicine has changed dramatically from twenty years ago, so the field that you would enter today is different from those of previous generations.

It is an unfortunate fact that medical practitioners are increasingly forced to deal with issues that take away time from their patients. While long hours have been a reality in medicine from the beginning, newer issues such as malpractice concerns and managed care bureaucracy weigh heavily on the mind of every physician. Medical students and residents aren't subject to these worries during their learning years, but they do have challenges of their own to face.

There should be no doubt that medical training will be one of the hardest tasks you ever undertake. It will change you as a person. Medical training is infamous for turning idealists into cynics. Medical students and residents have a higher rate of depression compared to the average student population. A large part of this has to do with the grueling system of training, as well as the realities of the emotionally difficult side of medicine on the hospital wards. Aside from trying to keep up academically with the overwhelming volume of material in the first two years, it is the years spent in the hospital as a medical student and resident that will test your limits of dedication, perseverance and intellect. There are many programs throughout the United States that expect residents to function at their best even after thirty-two sleepless hours on call. Patients will not always be grateful for your medical advice and attention, and may leave you wondering how you are helping them at all. And, perhaps most challenging of all, losing a patient that you had battled to keep alive for days will leave you feeling spent. It is in these hours that your original motivations for entering medicine will sustain you. **Passion is the fuel that will drive you when your body and mind will be exhausted**. By trusting themselves to your care, your patients don't deserve any less. And neither do you.

Who applies to Medical School?

Contrary to popular belief, medical school isn't reserved with seats only for academic geniuses. You do have to be an outstanding candidate, but this is defined in many ways. All medical schools are committed to the belief that educational opportunities should be available to all qualified persons without regard to race, creed, color, age, sex, religion, marital status, handicap or national origin.

Admissions Committees are looking for a diverse group of students to fill their seats. There will be a handful of academically brilliant individuals, but shining grades are no guarantee of acceptance either. A well-rounded individual who has shown distinction beyond academics will always make a better candidate than someone who has little aptitude beyond books. While you do need to meet the minimum academic requirements for each medical school, a unique characteristic that shows your dedication, either to sports, arts, humanities, or any field for that matter will set you apart from the thousands of other applicants. Since the variety of careers in the medical profession is so diverse, medical schools are seeking students with different strengths. The type of person that chooses to pursue a field like Neurosurgery, as defined by their personality, motivation and skills, varies from someone who decides to become a psychiatrist. The Admissions Committee is keenly aware of the need to balance the medical class based on the students' abilities to contribute in different ways to medicine. This means that there isn't just one definition of the ideal medical school candidate. As long as the basic requirements are met, two candidates from different walks of life, who may appear to have little in common, can both make for superb future doctors.

I was a little starstruck the first day of medical school. I met a student who had been an Olympic Rower, another who was a nationally acclaimed pianist, a third who was the youngest ever science graduate in the history of the university. But I also met a 34 year old mother of two who was changing careers, a 32 year old ex-pilot, an army reservist, an ex-nurse, a cancer survivor and many others like me who had gone straight from high school to university for an undergraduate degree, and then on to medical school.

The proportion of female medical students is increasing, and now accounts for slightly more than half of all admissions. The number of single parents, physically disabled students and second career students is also steadily increasing. Some may have worked previously in the healthcare field as a physician's assistant, nurse, physiotherapist or emergency medical technician. A small number of candidates will have attained a Masters degree or PhD prior to medical school.

Don't worry if the thought of death or sight of blood makes you faint. I have several colleagues who had such episodes in the first few weeks of medical school. One collapsed the first two times she stepped into the gross anatomy lab for cadaver dissection. Another felt lightheaded and had to excuse herself from her first surgical encounter. Another managed to draw my blood expertly on his first attempt, but fell straight to the ground as I inserted a butterfly needle into his vein. However, all recovered quickly, and are now either Family Practice or Surgical residents.

A significant number of colleagues in my class were admitted during their second attempt at medical school. **Your ability to make it into medical school depends largely on your determination.** If you have the conviction that medicine is the right field for you, you are already halfway there. The remaining will require some planning, and it's never too early to start.

Final Thoughts

Medicine is one of the oldest and most noble of professions. It stands as one of the giant pillars in the history of our world. The lives of countless millions have been improved through breakthroughs in this field. And this service to humanity continues everyday, in each doctor's office throughout the world. Healing is a privilege that patients entrust into our hands. Despite the rapidly changing face of medicine, the role of a doctor will remain the same - to console and treat, and to ultimately provide relief from suffering. It is a field for anyone dedicated to improving the lives of others. If you are thinking about a career in medicine, it is important to be aware of your motivations and passion for medicine at this stage. The remainder of this book will guide you towards directing your own path to becoming a doctor.

Chapter 2: Planning Ahead in High School

"The best preparation for tomorrow is to do today's work superbly well."
- Sir William Osler, first Professor of Medicine at John Hopkins University

It is often said that luck is the meeting of preparation with opportunity. For the medical school hopeful, opportunities are abundant. There are approximately 17,000 medical school positions available each year, with an increased number of seats on the horizon due to concerns of upcoming physician shortages. While there is no doubt that the competition is intense, always remember that not all candidates are equal. The students who consistently rise to the top are the ones who are thoroughly prepared and consistent in their achievements. They have put a lot of thought into developing themselves into well-balanced and interesting candidates. And to help fulfill the aspiration of entering medical school, there is no greater asset than time. This chapter focuses on specific strategies that high school students can use to start on the path towards medical school. It contains information on the early options available for pursuing a medical education following high school, and suggestions on choosing an undergraduate degree.

Options in High School

If you are already contemplating medicine as a high school student, congratulations on your early start. You have more alternatives available to you now than you will in college. Making a career decision is a very daunting task. You may not be sure about the abilities needed to become a doctor, and whether you are right for the field. To overcome these hurdles, you can start building a strong foundation by first maximizing your academic potential. This involves setting efficient study skills and striving to achieve the best grades possible. Second, seek extracurricular experiences that will encourage you to develop a wide range of interests. Examples include public speaking, participating in sports, developing artistic skills or getting involved in student organizations. Third, start looking for opportunities to work in healthcare settings. This can range from volunteering to shadowing physicians in the hospital. And lastly, examine your motivating factors and influences closely. By following these points, you will set the basis for a strong academic career both in high school and beyond, develop versatile skills, and gain firsthand experience in the healthcare field.

There are two broad categories of options available at the high school level: pursuing medicine directly from high school or applying to medicine once you have completed some college courses. It can be a difficult decision to decide on a permanent career choice at this stage, and shouldn't be taken lightly. Let's explore the first option.

Gaining a Diverse Education Prior to Medical School

You may be interested in pursuing a broader education before applying to medicine. For example, you might have an interest in Theatre or Psychology, and would like to take some courses in this area first. Or, like many students, you are not quite sure what fields interest you just yet. While medicine remains a possible career choice, you also want to look at Pharmacy, Economics or International Business.

The best option for students with multiple interests is to seek a varied education initially. Medical schools are no longer solely interested in candidates who have devoted themselves to sciences or a pre-med curriculum, so you won't be penalized for taking courses outside the pure sciences. They would rather attract students with unique interests, backgrounds and talents. Above all, they prefer candidates who have considered all their career options before deciding to dedicate themselves to the medical profession. This reflects a level of maturity that is necessary to pursuing a medical education.

If the above profile matches your interests, an undergraduate degree program, whether it is in arts, sciences or applied sciences will allow you to keep the option of medical school open while exploring other fields. You are in good company with this decision, as the majority of medical students complete an undergraduate degree prior to entering medical school.

From High School to Med School

The second option requires an exclusive commitment to medicine from high school itself. You might have outstanding academic credentials, and have weighed all your career options. You have discussed your decision with your family, career counselor and mentors. By this time, you should have spent significant hours volunteering in health-related and patient-centered programs. The hospital should be a familiar place to you, either because of your volunteer efforts or time spent shadowing doctors in various specialties. You have spoken to as many professionals in the healthcare field as you could, and also called up medical schools and asked to speak with medical students to have a better idea about medical school and training. If you are truly this prepared, then there are options available for medical training directly from high school.

These include entry into Combined Medical School programs, Combined Osteopathic Medical School programs, as well as seeking a medical education outside North America.

1. Combined Medical School Programs

BS/MD and BA/MD programs combine the Bachelor of Sciences or Arts and Doctor of Medicine degrees into a shorter or similar length of study, often 6-8 years. The advantage of these programs is that they eliminate some of the competition you would face if applying as an undergraduate, as you would be guaranteed medical training as long as good grades are maintained during the Bachelors degree. This is also a good option for students interested in medical research, as a significant component of some combined programs focuses on research prior to clinical training. In many programs, students begin participating in medical school classes, conferences and activities during the premedical years. An undergraduate degree program and a medical school program that are designed to complement each other may help to ease the transition to medical school. Additionally, the cost of a medical education is lowered if the coursework is completed within 6 years instead of 8. Institutions differ in the Medical College Admission Test (MCAT) requirement prior to entry into the first year medical class.

There are certain disadvantages to such programs also. First, this route may not allow full exploration of personal areas of interest, as electives will be eliminated in favor of completing the degree in a shorter period of time. Therefore, you may not get a chance to thoroughly explore other career or academic options. Second, you may find yourself committed for your entire educational endeavor to a program that doesn't suit your learning style or meet your intellectual needs. And third, the program may not provide an easy option of changing to another medical school or career without sacrificing the years of study already completed.

It is imperative to research the programs well before committing yourself. Speak with recent graduates or enrolled students. Educate yourself about the syllabus. **It can be tempting to complete the study of medicine in a shorter time frame, but it is far more important to be certain about your career decision.**

Proper research, self-reflection and exposure to the medical field will prove invaluable in making your decision.

Admissions criteria for the combined programs varies among schools, but generally include superior achievement on the Scholastic Aptitude Tests I and II in Math, Writing and Science, and in course work in English, Math, Physics, Biology and Chemistry. Foreign language, Calculus and Social Sciences may be required as well. ACT scores may be acceptable in lieu of SAT scores at some schools.

See **Appendix A** for a list of the medical colleges that offer a combined Bachelor of Science/Doctor of Medicine and/or Bachelor of Arts/Doctor of Medicine degrees for high school students.

2. Combined Osteopathic Medical School Programs

A second and less traditional option for high school students considering a combined undergraduate and medical degree program is an osteopathic medical education. Osteopathic medicine is a holistic system of healthcare which has a slightly different philosophy from traditional western, or allopathic, medicine. Its practices are based on the belief that a misalignment of the body's muscles and skeletal structure can lead to ill health. Unless altered by osteopathic manipulation, the body will remain impeded in its ability to heal itself. Health education and disease prevention receive special emphasis in an osteopathic school. Osteopathic physicians can qualify to practice allopathic medicine in the same way as any traditional medical graduate by writing the required licensing exams. Refer to Chapter 8 for more information.

There are twenty schools of osteopathic medicine in the United States, and graduates go on to complete internships and residencies either in osteopathic medicine or traditional allopathic medicine. Graduates attain a DO degree at the end of their medical school training. A large number of osteopathic graduates tend to practice in general medicine, such as Family Practice, Internal Medicine and Pediatrics. However, they are not limited to these fields, and can pursue Cardiology, Surgery, Intensive Care medicine or any specialty of their interest. There are presently 47,000 DO's licensed to practice in the U.S., comprising five percent of doctors in the country.

Some osteopathic medical schools offer combined Bachelor of Sciences and Doctor of Osteopathic Medicine training, requiring a total of seven years of education. Certain colleges offer a combined Bachelor of Science, Doctor of Osteopathic Medicine and Masters in Public Health degree, requiring eight years of education.

The admission requirements vary from school to school, but tend to require less competitive grade point averages and MCAT scores for admission. Tuitions range considerably among schools. It can be as low as $6,500 for in state students to a high of $45,000 for out of state students. Some colleges do not give preference to state residents, and charge annual fees in the range of $20,000 to $30,000. Osteopathic schools require a letter of recommendation from a DO, so students should seek clinical exposure prior to application. Combined programs require undergraduate coursework in the first three years, and only allow advancement to medical school if grade point cut-offs are met.

For information on Osteopathic Medicine, contact:

American Association of Colleges of Osteopathic Medicine (AACOM)
5550 Friendship Blvd., Suite 310
Chevy Chase MD 20815-7231
Tel: (301) 968-4190
www.aacom.org

3. Foreign Medical Education

A small number of American high school students choose to study at foreign medical schools each year. Some countries accept applications from high school as well as college students, and require 6 years of study. They do not offer undergraduate degrees, however, so an opportunity at a broad based education would be lost for high school graduates. Competition for medical seats at these schools is much lower than in the U.S., and the MCAT is not required. Tuition tends to be comparable with a private U.S. medical education.

Just as there are the advantages of completing a medical education in a shorter period of time and eliminating competition for a medical school position in the U.S., there are significant disadvantages also. First, adjustment from high school to college requires getting accustomed to a new environment and a new level of independence. A network of family and friends often cushions the hardships of challenging experiences, but these support systems would be sorely lacking in another country. This is much more pronounced if the student is unfamiliar with the language and customs of the country. Many foreign schools do not offer English curriculums, so students are expected to spend one year acquiring the necessary language skills before beginning the medical curriculum.

Second, many foreign schools do not have the same curriculum, level of clinical teaching facilities and diagnostic equipment available in North America. This will be a significant disadvantage when you return to practice in the U.S. Additionally, not all medical schools are recognized as having acceptable teaching facilities. Only institutions included in the *World Directory of Medical Schools* (http://www.who.int), published by the World Health Organization, or the *International Medical Education Directory* (http://imed.ecfmg.org) are recognized as accredited foreign medical schools.

Third, disreputable foreign medical schools have been known to close down their facilities or have their credentials revoked while students are still in the program. The closure of some schools has led to licensing difficulties even for graduates of previous years when they try to obtain a medical license in the United States.

These are only a few disadvantages that high school students seeking a medical education in a foreign country may face. For a full discussion of foreign medical schools, see Chapter 9. Despite intense competition for U.S. medical schools, a candidate who prepares well, and fulfills the criteria required by American medical schools will most likely succeed in obtaining a position. Remember that the odds are presently one in two. A better option for high school students seeking a faster route would be to consider the combined 6 and 7 year programs available in the U.S.

Strategies for Planning Ahead in High School

Regardless of the path that you may decide to take to medical school, there are specific strategies that can be utilized in high school to begin your preparation. An early start will allow you to appraise the qualities that are considered necessary in the making of a doctor, and match your aptitudes to them. The final result will be an informed and personal career choice. Exposing yourself continually to your goals will bring you one step closer to reaching them, so photocopy the following table and tape it to a location that you frequent often, such as your study desk.

1. Research your way to success

Contact your prospective university programs, and inquire into the courses and grades required for undergraduate or combined program admission. Schedule an interview with your high school career counselor to ensure that you have all the necessary courses in your timetable.

2. Keep your options open

Most medical schools require 1st year university level Physics, Chemistry, Biology, English and Math. Most will also require 2nd year Chemistry. Build a strong foundation by taking these courses in high school.

3. Consider advanced level courses

If your high school offers an honors or advanced level course in the above subject areas, consider taking them. They will cover material you will be taught in your first year college courses, therefore allowing higher grades in college. You do not necessarily have to accept credit for the advanced level course once you are in college though. Medical schools will only look at your undergraduate, not high school, transcript. If you can attain a higher grade in first year Chemistry because you had already covered this material in high school, all the better!

4. Become an all-rounder

Medical schools are interested in candidates who have interests beyond pure sciences, and can talk intelligently on a number of different topics. If you can demonstrate that your abilities include excelling in academic work as well as extracurricular activities, the more interesting you will be as an applicant. Consider involvement in drama, sports, arts, music, humanities.

5. Seek medical volunteer opportunities

Look for volunteering programs within your local hospital and nursing homes. Patients have a lot to teach us, and this is your opportunity to get to know patients as individuals, and see medicine through their eyes. You will also be better able to judge your decision of pursuing a medical career, and will be exposed to allied health care fields at the same time, such as physiotherapy and nursing. Teamwork is an important aspect of working in hospitals, so start building your communication skills early.

6. Find a mentor

Seek out physicians in the community who are willing to be mentors. Learn from them by spending a day in the hospital or their clinics. Discuss the challenges they face in their practices, as well as the advantages of their specialty. If you don't know many physicians, start with your own doctor. Or phone your childhood pediatrician. Tell them you want to be just like them. They won't refuse.

Guidelines on Choosing an Undergraduate Degree

It is a common misperception that medical schools only accept candidates with strong Math and Science skills. In fact, the majority of medical schools do not require a specific degree or program of study for entrance into medical studies. This is different from years ago when pre-med programs were abundant. The problem was that candidates who did not get accepted into medical school could not do much with their pre-medical education. Now, the focus has shifted, and schools are looking for well-rounded individuals with diverse interests. They emphasize a broad-based education that balances scholarly pursuits with your special interests and talents. This means that you can choose to do a traditional Bachelors Degree in Sciences, or even an Arts, Pharmacy, Political Science or Engineering Degree. I had a colleague who had a degree in Music in my medical class. As long as you maintain a high grade point average, your choices are only limited by your interests.

Consult the *Medical School Admissions Requirements* in your library for more information on acceptance rates into medical school for different course majors.

The majority of medical school applicants choose a Science degree, as it becomes easier to fulfill the pre-requisite requirements within the program. There are many, however, who choose an alternate degree and fulfill their pre-requisite requirements through electives. It takes some creativity at times, but it is certainly possible. Each medical school will have slightly different criteria. It is up to you to research their requirements before choosing your undergraduate program of study. You should also consult with a premedical counselor, if one is available, about your choice of courses.

Electives in your degree program are a great way of learning more about the field of medicine, such as courses on the History of Medicine or Biomedical Ethics, offered as arts electives.

I chose to do a Bachelor's degree in Sciences, with emphasis on Chemistry and Asian Studies. My degree fulfilled all medical school pre-requisites, and I also got an opportunity to learn about Asian history, poetry and learn a new language. I took additional electives in History of Medicine, International Health, Biomedical ethics and a course on Latin roots of medical terminology.

If, however, you choose not to delve too deeply into medicine while completing your Bachelors degree, and prefer to leave it for medical school, use your electives wisely in making yourself a more desirable and informed candidate. Admissions Committees are interested in students who have worked to develop strong 'people' skills, such as communication, and show an understanding of ethical issues, cultural diversity and international health awareness. For a broad, liberal education, consider taking courses in the Humanities and Social Sciences such as Psychology, Anthropology, Philosophy and Literature. These bodies of knowledge provide a unique slant on human behavior that isn't found in medical school.

As you consider the various majors and courses, try to keep other potential careers open. After learning more about medicine, you may decide that it is not the right field for you, either due to its training requirements, length of study, financial burdens or level of competition. If the idea of making a difference by helping patients through illnesses has drawn you towards healthcare,there are other fields that can provide the same opportunities. Additional careers that carry the title of doctor are optometry, podiatry, chiropracty, dentistry and veterinary medicine. In addition, consider other occupations in the health services. Rather than pursue a basic science degree first, you could decide to train as a physician assistant, nurse practitioner, pharmacist, physical therapist or nutritionist during your undergraduate years, and then apply to medical school. You will not only have gained considerable experience in the medical field, but will have a reliable career in case medical school doesn't remain a viable option.

Final Thoughts

High school is the best time for considering different career choices. Nothing helps more than working directly with patients, so make this the priority when exploring volunteer opportunities. Students interested in medicine can save a lot of time and frustration (and their parent's bank accounts) by exploring medicine early. The numerous options available at this stage - from combined programs in allopathic and osteopathic medical schools, to foreign medical education - make high school a critical decision-making time. Students who prefer to leave their career decision until they've had a chance to enjoy the college years will still benefit by paying attention to the criteria sought by medical schools. As an undergraduate student, there are more strategies they will be able to use to stand out in the applications process for medical school, and these are discussed next.

Chapter 3: Strategies for Undergraduate Students

"Education is not the filling of a pail, but the lighting of a fire."
- W.B. Yeats

The college years are a time that is looked forward to with much anticipation as well as apprehension. It brings a different environment, with a new sense of independence and responsibility. Academic expectations will increase. The workload will be vastly different from high school. You will be exposed to people and situations that you may have never encountered before. And it will soon be time to embark on a decisive career path.

In addition to providing an educational background for employment, the undergraduate years provide the best opportunity for exposure to a variety of academic fields, and help identify unique aptitudes and interests. It is the right time to seriously contemplate studying medicine, as medical schools are interested in your accomplishments at this juncture in life. Since medical training requires a minimum of three years of undergraduate coursework, you can use the time to develop yourself into a strong applicant. Even if becoming a doctor didn't strike you until you were in the second, third or even fourth year of your degree, strategic planning and the right guidance can put you on the fast track towards medical school.

The first step to becoming a qualified candidate is to gain a superb understanding of the qualities sought by Admissions Committees. Let's begin by taking a look at their requirements.

What are Medical Schools Looking For?

Medical schools will always draw eager and bright minds to its doors. It is also a certainty that the number of applications will exceed available spots each year. Maximizing your chances of admission requires careful thought and preparation. And to plan ahead effectively, you need to have an understanding of the academic and non-academic criteria for admission.

Academic Criteria:

Most schools require at least three years of college coursework prior to medical school admission. Pre-requisite courses that need to be completed include first year level Calculus, English, Physics, Biology, and Chemistry (with labs), and second year level Organic Chemistry and Biochemistry. There are variations among schools, however, and it is crucial to check the admissions requirements of all medical schools that interest you. Statistics, Humanities, Social Sciences and Behavioral Sciences are additional requirements at some institutions. To assess academic ability, Admissions Committees will look at trends in grades from year to year, overall grade point average in all undergraduate and graduate courses, grade point average in the Sciences, and grade point average in prerequisite courses.

Scores achieved on the MCAT are just as important as the grade point average in your undergraduate courses. The MCAT is a standardized test aimed at assessing academic ability and critical thinking skills. It is comprised of sections on Verbal Reasoning, Physical and Biological Sciences, and two writing samples.

Students should aim to have a grade point average greater than 3.5/4.0 to be competitive for medical school admission

Non-academic Criteria:

Over the last decade, schools have placed increasing importance on the non-academic qualifications of candidates. Admission committees use many tools in the application process to measure these qualities:
- Personal Statement - an 800-900 word essay that allows evaluation of motivations, diversity in background, individual interests and abilities, creativity, exposure to medicine, and social responsibility such as volunteer work.

- Reference letters - recommendations from professors, supervisors or physicians which allow a perspective on your level of maturity, integrity, leadership ability, achievements and research experience.
- Personal Interviews - a face to face interview with members of the Admissions Committee which allows an assessment of interpersonal skills, confidence level, self-knowledge, commitment to medicine, sincerity, honesty and empathy.

The Essential CARE Mantra

The process of getting into medical school can be greatly simplified by focusing on the basic academic and non-academic requirements. By simplifying these basic elements into a plan, you can then start taking steps to implement it. This book suggests a method that is foolproof in satisfying every demand of the Admissions Committee. The CARE mantra provides the focus that you will need to develop into a well-rounded, outstanding candidate for medical school. So what is it?

It is an easy mnemonic that you can use to keep your goals foremost in mind while planning ahead. When the Admissions Committee peruses your application, they will look for four main elements: Character, Academics, Research and Extracurricular activities.

Character:

All medical schools will look for clues to your character and personality, first in your personal essay, then in your reference letters, and finally in your interviews. Medicine is a profession where your patient's well-being comes foremost. You will deal with patients from all battlegrounds of life, who will have life stories that you would never have heard about had you pursued another profession. Patients will be at their most vulnerable in your hands. Do you have a sense of compassion when you see others in pain and suffering? Do you have the ability to put your own motivations and feelings aside and focus on other's needs? Are you a mature and tolerant person? Would others say you have passion and integrity?

While character takes a lifetime to develop, the actions that we take every single day reflect who we are at our core. Seek out experiences in your life that build your character. This can range from helping at a soup kitchen to volunteering with mentally challenged children, to reading to the elderly at a nursing home. Take initiative in projects that aim to better the lives of those around you. Take a leadership role in a project. You cannot help but be changed by these experiences.

Academics:

A consistently solid academic track record is vital to your application. Medical schools will have different minimum grade point average requirements, but incoming students often have a higher average than the minimum requested. Focus on the prerequisite courses that the medical school has specified. Your performance in these courses gives them a benchmark in comparing you with other candidates.

Courses like Organic Chemistry are considered the 'weeding out' course. In any first year undergraduate class, the number of people considering medical school is fairly high. After second year Organic Chemistry, however, a substantial number of students will have altered their career plans on receiving a dismal grade. Avoid this pitfall by taking additional tutorial classes if you aren't confident in your abilities. Spend extra time reviewing, and do it daily. While the subject matter of Organic Chemistry has little to do with practicing clinical medicine later, a failing grade will make all the difference in whether or not you get into medical school.

Research:

If you are a masters or PhD candidate and are choosing to apply to medical school now, chances are that you have extensive experience with research already. For the remaining candidates, involvement in research projects will rank you very favorably. In some prestigious schools, it has even become an unwritten requirement. Needless to say, publication in a journal or experience with presentations regarding your research will give you an advantage. If you don't have experience already, consider finding a part-time or summer job within your Department with a Professor. Also, contact the closest medical school, and inquire into the possibility of doing research with one of their faculty members. Research experience doesn't have to be in the scientific field. Allow your interests to lead you. There are many research grants and opportunities available within colleges and universities, and it is up to you to use them to further your goals.

My research experiences were outside the pure sciences. My first research exposure occurred during the summer between the second and third year of university. I was hired to conduct ethnographic research on pioneers for a museum. I conducted interviews, searched national archives for photographs and information, and set up a museum exhibit based on the information. The second research project occurred in a community hospital the following summer. The goal was to review patient data records and target areas of quality improvement for the hospital. For example, one aspect involved looking at the time cardiac patients spent in Emergency Rooms before receiving life-saving treatment for an acute heart attack. I had no special medical knowledge prior to being hired. In fact, my supervisor had been looking for a medical student. I found out later that I was chosen for my enthusiasm and keen interest in the project. Though I had never done so before at an interview, I showed my future supervisor a copy of my university transcript to substantiate that I had a good track record and the academic aptitude to complete the project. She ended up writing one of my letters of recommendation for medical school.

Extracurricular Activities:

A candidate with diverse interests and experiences always makes for a memorable applicant. Extracurricular activities can include volunteer experiences, unique adventures, leadership in student group activities, or other skills and interests. All volunteer experiences are useful, but try to gain experience within a healthcare setting. Hospitals run numerous volunteer programs. Programs that will allow you to participate in patient education will let you work with patients, and provide valuable experience with communication skills. Also seek out community centers and nursing homes that may have programs suited to your interests. Examples include volunteer support for groups like battered women, traumatic brain-injured patients, Alzheimer's patients, and so forth.

An important point to keep in mind is that these activities cannot replace the value of good grades on your transcript. If your academic standing is at risk of suffering due to over-commitment to extracurricular activities, your immediate action should be to shift focus back to studies. Choose extracurricular activities with some thought. Focus on the ones where you can make the most difference, and those that enhance your personal growth.

Over a period of four years, I worked as a volunteer in the Obstetrics division of a hospital, assisted Physical and Occupational therapists at an extended care nursing home, and tutored special needs grade school children.

The CARE mantra will help to strengthen you as an applicant from all fronts. Keep it in mind whenever you are about to initiate a new project. Ask yourself if the undertaking will take you closer to your goals. If it doesn't fit the mantra, chances are that it won't. If so, can you afford to spend time away from pursuing your dream? All choices have consequences, so be selective in what you decide to place in your life.

Strategies for Planning Ahead in College

Medical schools look at the following five pieces of information when assessing an application: the candidate's GPA, MCAT score, Letters of Recommendation, Personal Essay and lastly, the 'distinctive' factor, which can be unique features in your application such as clinical, research or life experience.

Therefore, your goals during the undergraduate experience will be to:
1. maintain a high grade point average
2. become familiar with MCAT subject material well ahead of time
3. initiate early contact with professors and physicians for future letters of recommendation
4. develop or nurture diverse interests
5. gain clinical and research experience

There are specific strategies that can be used to meet all these objectives. Let's go through each one.

*   **Plan your courses**

This requires that you look into the prerequisites needed for the medical schools of your choice. If you are in a Science program, you may be able to fit in all the first year requirements easily, such as Biology, Chemistry, English and Math. For non-Science majors, use your electives to fulfill the required criteria. Courses such as Biochemistry, Genetics and Microbiology aren't often required, but can help immensely when writing the MCAT. When scheduling courses, be aware of your limitations. If Biology is a weak subject, you may want to schedule this course for a semester that has a lighter load. The first semester of first year of college is often the most difficult. The adjustment period will be demanding, and the extra independence gained in college can interfere with your academic goals. Discuss your concerns with an academic advisor, and develop a strategy that allows you to handle the more difficult classes in turn rather than simultaneously.

*   **Attend all lectures and labs**

This may seem obvious, but it never failed to surprise me how some of my classes seemed to fill up right before exams. Students who neglect to put in work during the semester and try to make up for it by attending the last few sessions will always be left scrambling. Instructors often provide tips for the final exam throughout the semester rather than just at the end.

- **Read ahead**

Lectures will make much more sense if you have some knowledge of the topic being covered. Dedicate half an hour the night prior to the lecture to skimming the appropriate chapters. Try some questions at the end of the chapter. Even if you end up solving just half the problem, you will be much further ahead than your class-mates.

- **Consolidate knowledge on a daily and weekly basis**

Review the lecture at the end of the day. Make notes on the sides of the pages and create a summary page. Add in information from your textbook to make the points clearer. At the end of the week, review your summary pages. This process often takes less than twenty minutes, and saves hours at the end of the semester when you will be studying for not one but up to five different subjects.

- **Use tutorials or instructor office hours**

Professors are often willing to help point out the key points of lectures and labs that they expect you to master for the exam. Use their expertise to direct your study efforts. This is also a good way of acquainting yourself with potential refer-ees for letters of recommendation for medical school, and seeking summer or part-time research positions in their labs.

- **Study from old exams**

Usually, the best predictor of the difficulty level and material tested on your final exam are the old exams. Find out where you can obtain past copies, and go over them thoroughly. There is nothing more satisfying than finding similar questions on your exam and answering them confidently.

- **Choose the best instructors**

Some colleges publish a ranking of the best professors in each field, based on stu-dent choice. Try to find the ones who are enthusiastic about the subject and are known for their ability to present the material in a student friendly manner. You can also sit in on the first few lectures of different instructors, and choose the one best suited to your learning style. Use the option given by your college of drop-ping any course within the first two weeks without incurring a 'Withdrawal' on your transcript.

- **Be wary of auditing difficult courses**

Prospective medical school students often ask about the possibility of auditing dif-ficult undergraduate courses in the summer. Auditing is an option at colleges, which means attending class lectures, but being exempt from doing assignments or writing the final exam. Students may choose this option prior to enrolling as a registered student the following semester in a difficult course, such as Organic

Chemistry. The benefit is gaining familiarity with the coursework in a stress-free setting prior to taking the course officially. The disadvantages, however, may outweigh the advantages for a prospective medical student. Colleges won't assign a grade to the student or give credit for an audited course, but they may list the course on the official transcript with the notation 'Audit' next to it. Any medical school reviewing the applicant's transcript is likely to make a note of this, and it may be viewed as nothing less than a sly way of gaining a better grade.

- **Inquire into resources for medical school applicants**

Resources may include the pre-med office, which often keeps books on different medical schools and their application procedures. Your premedical school advisor is also an excellent resource for answering questions about the application process, and for guiding your undergraduate work.

- **Seek out medical mentors**

The first mentor should ideally be a physician. Ask for opportunities to shadow in the hospital and clinic, and gain contacts with physicians in other specialties also. They will be able to provide you with a glimpse of what your future life will be like. Different fields of medicine are quite diverse in work responsibilities, work hours, level of interaction with patients and academic/research components, so try to gain exposure to as many specialties as possible. The second mentor can be a medical student or resident. They can be invaluable for advice when practicing for medical school interviews, and for painting a picture of what your immediate future will be like when you are undergoing medical training. If you aren't acquainted with one personally, call up a medical school and ask to be put in touch with a student. First and second year students have better schedules than the senior years, and are more likely to be open to such requests.

- **Strengthen leadership skills**

Actively participate in an arena that interests you. Take on responsibilities that demand interaction with peers in a leadership capacity. For example, organize a student group which aims to improve social awareness on a topic of your interest, or lead a food bank drive.

- **Pick up a book on the MCAT a year in advance**

Familiarize yourself with the subject matter and objectives of the exam. Take note of test strategies. As you learn those topics in Chemistry, Biology and Physics lectures, attempt the questions on the practice exams. Your comfort level with the format and types of questions will be an advantage when it comes time to start studying seriously in the third year.

- **Look for opportunities in local and international health projects**

Student groups on campus, such as the pre-med club, international health club and social awareness groups often offer opportunities for involvement with health projects. These may range from educating high school students about healthy lifestyle choices to organizing campaigns for awareness of sexually transmitted diseases on campus. Your pre-med advisor may be able to advise you regarding overseas opportunities also. These projects take place in developing nations and focus on educating communities and providing medical service. It's a great way to gain a unique perspective on international health and different cultures.

Tip:

Various organizations are dedicated to recruiting volunteers to locations such as Peru, India, El Salvador, Argentina, Bangladesh, Brazil, China, Cambodia, Mexico, Israel, Tanzania, Thailand, Romania, and locally within the United States. Their goal is to provide humanitarian aid through education, distribute supplies such as wheelchairs, books, shoes and other essentials to orphanages, assist youth in learning trades, build clinics, and other similar compassionate missions. For those interested in volunteering in medical clinics, there are opportunities for working with physicians. Level of assistance would range from changing bandages to taking blood pressures, weighing babies and providing education on hygiene and health maintenance.

Some of the following organizations are linked to the United Nations and have the approval of the U.S. Congress. Missions can be as short as 1 to 2 weeks, or last as long as two years, depending on location and need. It is advisable to research each organization thoroughly prior to any involvement.

Airline Ambassadors International www.airlineambassadors.org	Pediatrician's for Central America's Children 516-663-9409
Peace Corps www.peacecorps.gov 1-800-424-8580	Worldteach www.worldteach.org 1-800-483-2240

• **Choose part-time work wisely**

Many students need to work while enrolled in full-time studies. Let your work experience help in your application by choosing a field that adds to your bid for medical school. Working in a hospital or other healthcare setting is a good choice, but don't feel limited. For example, tutorial work with children and high school or college students will develop your skills in communicating and teaching. After all, the root of the word doctor means 'one who teaches'. As long as the nature of the work relates to the CARE criteria, your part-time job will serve to sustain you financially for the present and also help make a doctor out of you. The Admissions Committee will recognize your ability to handle outside pressures while managing a full course load.

I held two part-time jobs during the undergraduate years, which required a time commitment of 20 hours each week. The first was as a Computer Tutor to international students on campus, and the second as a Student Assistant in the Department of Continuing Medical Education. In the latter, I helped organize mailings and assembled conference packages for physicians. The first job helped to demonstrate diverse skills (skilled computer knowledge, teaching ability) and the second showed my interest in the medical arena. Both jobs were flexible and allowed me to set my own schedule. This proved invaluable during exam periods.

The Best Time to Apply for Medical School

Once you have worked to meet the academic and non-academic criteria outlined by medical schools, it will be time to start contacting medical schools. The best time to apply will depend on your circumstances. For the undergraduate student, approximately 90 percent of candidates choose to submit applications for medical school during the beginning of the third year of university. This would allow them to start medical school following graduation. For candidates considering entering medical school after three years of undergraduate studies, they will need to apply during the second year of studies.

It is important to time the writing of the MCAT with your application date. The MCAT is administered in April and August of each year. Many students opt to take it in April. In case they don't perform well, there is still the option of retaking the exam in August and being within the appropriate time frame for entry the following year for most schools. For a discussion of the advantages and disadvantages of taking the exam in April or August, refer to Chapter 5.

For candidates who have already attained their undergraduate degree or are changing careers, the best time to apply would be once they have gained significant experience with healthcare and patients, either through volunteer experiences or previous work experiences. They would also need to ensure that the pre-requisite academic and MCAT requirements have been met. Candidates need to demonstrate a clear and focused commitment to becoming a physician in order to be a successful applicant.

TIP:

Meet with the Dean of Admissions at least one year prior to applying for medical school. Schedule an interview and present yourself as a future applicant. Ask for advice on elective course choices that can help you be a better doctor in the long run, especially for topics that may not be well covered in medical school. I was advised to take a Nutrition course by the Dean due to skimpy coverage of this topic in medical school. You have accomplished two tasks by doing this: the Dean may remember you during your medical school interviews, and you have made yourself a stronger candidate by committing yourself to becoming a better doctor.

Final Thoughts

Planning ahead is critical for success as a medical school applicant. Medical schools no longer desire a specific pre-med curriculum as an undergraduate degree. They are seeking individuals with unique and diverse backgrounds.

For an undergraduate student, focusing on the most important criteria sought by medical schools is key. By using the CARE mantra and the specific strategies outlined, a mediocre student can become an outstanding medical school candidate. The years spent preparing for medical school is an exciting time as well. Medical school is all-consuming, so use the undergraduate years to learn about yourself, expand your interests and organize your life. Before you know it, it will be time to start thinking about how to submit your application and pay for medical school.

Chapter 4: Applying to Medical School and Paying For It

"To be what we are, and to become what we are capable of becoming, is the only end of life."
- Robert Louis Stevenson

When the time comes to apply to medical school, filling out the forms will leave you gritting your teeth. Applicants need to fill out one initial primary application, then individual secondary applications sent out by the schools. It is easy to get overwhelmed at this stage, but the good part is that most questions are repetitive. The key is to spend a sufficient amount of time crafting your application, and then to remain organized once the admissions game begins. On average, each applicant applies to approximately ten to fifteen medical schools.

How Do I Apply to Medical School?

The process of applying has been simplified by the Association of American Medical Colleges (AAMC). The AAMC provides a central application service, called the American Medical College Application Service (AMCAS). There are 125 accredited medical schools in the United States, and students can apply to the majority of programs directly through the service. A listing of all the schools is provided at www.aamc.org.

The first step involves providing AMCAS with a completed application form and official transcript. The application form requests information on previous schools attended, grades, extracurricular activities, employment record, awards and accomplishments, and a personal statement. Medical schools will then contact you to fill out a secondary application and send in letters of recommendation. Some schools send secondary applications to every candidate, while others will screen the initial application before offering secondary applications to the most qualified students. The AMCAS application is available from May 1 of each year. Depending on the medical school, the deadline varies from October 15 to December 15. Schools that don't participate in AMCAS have their own timetables for the application process. The following schools need to be contacted directly for admissions information and materials. The schools that don't participate in AMCAS include:

Brown University
Columbia University
New York University School of Medicine
Texas A & M University System Health Science Center
Texas Tech University
University of Missouri - Kansas City
University of North Dakota School of Medicine
University of Texas - Galveston, Houston, San Antonio, Southwestern
(Applicants to UT Southwestern MD/PhD Program may apply through AMCAS; other UT Southwestern programs are ineligible)

It is in your best interest to apply early, as Admissions Committees begin reviewing applications soon after the schools begin accepting them. They will also offer interviews as they come across promising candidates during the review process. There may not be many spots left by the time late applications arrive. A disproportionately large number of applicants submit their packages on the last possible date, so take the early bird special to give your application a chance of standing out.

MCAT scores will be sent directly to medical schools through the MCAT service at your request. Medical schools will only request further materials and information from candidates in whom they have an interest. It is therefore imperative that your written submissions showcase your highest potential, as the Admissions Committee will only agree to an interview once they have sufficient evidence of your capabilities.

AMCAS can be contacted at:
American Medical College Application Service
Association of American Medical Colleges
2450 N Street NW Washington DC 20037-1123
http://www.aamc.org/students/amcas
amcas@aamc.org

The Early Decision Program

Approximately 90 medical schools offer the option of an early decision for applicants. Through this program, candidates can apply to only one school, and await an early decision. All application materials need to be submitted by August 1 to schools that participate in AMCAS, and decisions are announced on October 1. Deadlines vary for non-AMCAS schools. The offer of acceptance is binding, so the student is obliged to attend the school if accepted. If unsuccessful, the student then has the option of applying under the general admissions category to the same school, as well as submitting applications to other medical schools. Many programs have stipulations to their Early Decision Program, such as state residency requirements.

While the program can decrease the stress and traveling costs associated with applying to multiple schools, it does have a significant disadvantage. Students won't get an opportunity to pick and choose among scholarships and financial aid packages from other schools. Therefore, only students keenly interested in attending one particular medical school despite financial considerations should consider this program. If unsuccessful, students will find themselves rushing to submit their applications to other medical schools.

Important Dates in the Applications Process

- **May 1** - AMCAS application becomes available
- **August 1** - Early Decision Program deadline
- **October 15-December 15** - application deadlines for medical schools vary
- **March 15** -most acceptance and waitlist letters are mailed out
- **May 15** - final date for students with multiple acceptances to decide on a school; more spots open up and the second round of acceptance letters are mailed

Selecting Medical Schools

I must admit that choosing the right medical school was not high on my 'things to worry about' list when I was applying. I would have been happy just to be enrolled in a school that could add an MD next to my name. But as the decision process went on, and I started flying across the country to interview at different places, the need to create a priority list soon emerged.

Ultimately, the choice of the right medical school will depend on factors such as location, state residency, school environment, finances, school philosophy, preference for certain curriculums, student feedback, and any other personal preferences. Some factors will hold far more value for you than it does for the next candidate. As multiple schools start to offer acceptance letters, diligent research and prioritizing your needs will rescue you from making a random decision.

How to Choose Schools That Will Want You

If you haven't already done so, familiarize yourself with the Medical School Admissions Requirements published by the AAMC. The profiles of medical schools contain information obtained from each medical school in the United States and Canada. It outlines the criteria that schools are looking for, as well as statistics on the applicants that get accepted into these institutions. For example, it may show that 85% of enrolled students at a particular school are state residents. This is good news if you happen to be one also, but as an out-of-state resident, your chances of admission decline rapidly, regardless of your excellent qualifications.

Some schools state an interest in applicants with unique life experiences, or research experience. Some are partial to students who come from rural areas of a state. Due to the lack of physician providers in underserved areas of the country, medical schools have a vested interest in selecting candidates who are familiar with a rural lifestyle. Their hope is that these physicians will be more inclined to return to their home communities to practice medicine. Therefore, by matching your own strengths with those that the schools are seeking, you will dramatically increase your chances for acceptance.

How to Choose Schools That You Want

There is a choice of 125 allopathic medical schools in the United States. Consider the following criteria when narrowing your list of the choices:

- **Is location important?**

Personal motivations for remaining in a certain state might be a factor for you, particularly if there are family commitments. Consider the advantages and disadvantages of relocation, and always involve your spouse or significant other in the discussion. Research factors such as the cost of housing, and whether you may need a car to reach the training hospitals and clinics. If you have children and aren't familiar with the area, inquire about schools, daycare facilities and the safety of the neighborhoods.

- **Are you seeking a career in research, academics or clinical medicine?**

While all schools will offer the opportunity to train in all three areas, their focus and ability to provide the best education suited to your interests will be different. Look at the primary objectives of each school, and select the ones best suited to your career plans. The better able you are at defining your goals to the Admissions Committee, the easier it will be to rank highly with a school that matches those educational objectives.

- **Are you interested in a combined degree program?**

Many medical schools offer the opportunity of working towards an additional degree while completing your medical degree, such as a Masters in Public Health, J.D., MBA or PhD. See Chapter 7 for more information.

- **Are finances a consideration in your choice? What financial aid is available?**

Consider all your sources of financial help, including family loans or gifts, personal savings, federal and state student loan programs, and private loans. State school tuition may be considerably less than private schools, but it is also more competitive to gain admission. Debt reduction information for students is available from the individual financial aid offices. Inquire into scholarship programs. The range of financial aid in the form of scholarships from medical school or university funds varies greatly, from 3% to 100%. In addition to federal and state loan programs, research the eligibility criteria for merit and need-based awards.

- **Do you have a preference for learning styles?**

There are three major types of curriculums offered at medical schools. The traditional learning method focuses on a subject-based didactic learning system, with lectures as the main form of instruction. The separate fields of Pharmacology, Physiology, Pathology, Histology and Anatomy are covered in sequential order, with several weeks to months devoted to each topic. The second type is an organ based curriculum, where topics like Physiology, Pharmacology, and Pathology are taught with an organ as its focus. When learning about the brain, for example, the module would start with a few introductory basic science lectures, followed by labs in Neuroanatomy and Neurohistology. Drugs specific to the nervous system would be discussed in lectures and small learning groups. Lastly, clinical problems would be analyzed by integrating all this information. A newer and more innovative learning style stresses a problem-based learning system which minimizes lectures and emphasizes independent learning. The problem-based system puts the burden of gathering information on all aspects of a given problem on the student - from the basic sciences aspect to understanding its clinical implications. Most schools offer a combination of these learning systems. You may feel this factor isn't very important in your final decision, but given the amount of knowledge and the rapid pace at which it must be acquired during medical studies, identifying the learning style that suits you best should be given careful thought.

- **Do you prefer early clinical exposure?**

Certain schools offer exposure to patients as early as the first year. For example, you may spend a half day a week in a Family Practitioner's office during the first two years of medical school. Other schools offer structured exposure to patients through clinical skills courses, where students are taught history-taking and physical examination skills on a volunteer patient. For example, during Immunology Week, students would be introduced to a patient with an autoimmune condition, such as Systemic Lupus Erythematosus. Students would be expected to learn the basics of taking a focused history of the illness, and competently examine the patient, looking for the defining features of the disease.

- **What is the range of clinical exposure?**

Students rotate through different hospitals during the clinical years. Assess if there is adequate exposure to all socioeconomic groups of patients, as medicine is best learnt by listening to patients from different backgrounds. Inner city and tertiary care hospitals provide maximum exposure to trauma medicine, such as major motor vehicle accidents and gun shot wounds. VA hospitals and extended care facilities focus on treating chronic conditions, such as chronic obstructive pulmonary disease and heart disease.

- **Do you prefer a school that emphasizes primary care and prepares you for general community practice?**

If the thought of being a general practitioner or rural physician appeals to you, a school that provides a broader experience, with electives in rural and community medicine, may be of interest. Inquire into the educational philosophy of the school, as well as the percentage of medical students who choose general practice residencies following graduation.

- **Does the school offer national or international electives?**

The choice of electives at specific hospitals becomes important when considering residency choices. Often, students will choose to do one or two electives at a hospital where they hope to attain a residency position following graduation. This allows them to gain contacts with the clinical faculty, as well as to demonstrate their interest in being matched to that program.

International electives are also a popular choice among students. Several of my classmates chose to do research or clinical electives in locations such as Malawi, Hong Kong, India and South Africa. The rewards of exposure to international health are many. We often do not stop to consider that there are many parts of the world that do not have access to the medical knowledge, technology and medications that we take for granted in North America. The political and economic circumstances of the country are reflected in the health of its people. Physical and psychosocial illnesses seen in impoverished areas stem from the conflicts and famine that surround its citizens. An international medical experience holds the promise of profoundly changing your perspective and attitude, and may even lead you to discover a greater purpose in your professional life.

My own international elective experience was in the Fiji Islands in the South Pacific. I worked in the Internal Medicine department of an urban hospital for a month, and saw diseases that I hadn't even learnt about in my first three years of medical school. Who knew that some tropical fishes can cause respiratory collapse and death with just one swipe of their venomous tails? See Chapter 12 for my experiences in this developing island nation.

The Cost of a Medical Education

Total educational debt for the average medical student today is greater than $100,000. This figure includes both college and medical school loans.

The variation in tuition among different public and private medical schools, and among different states, can be astonishing. State residents usually qualify for a lower tuition rate, so financially-conscious applicants should give priority to their state schools when applying.

Annual medical school tuition and fees for a private education ranges from $10,000 to $40,000. For a public education, in-state resident tuition and fees ranges from $5,000 to $26,000 and out-of-state fees ranged from $30,000 to $37,000.

In addition to tuition, student will also have to consider their living expenses, books, equipment costs (stethoscope, ophthalmoscope, otoscope, computer), transportation, and student fees. In the second and fourth year, there are licensing exam fees. The fourth year will require additional funds for transportation to residency interviews.

It is an unfortunate fact that medical school costs are rising every year, and requires going into significant debt to obtain an education. However, there are many sources of help available for students.

Consider the following forms of financial aid:

• **Grants and Scholarships**
These should always be the first source of funding. They are awarded based on academic achievement or financial need. Contact the Financial Aid Office for qualification details and deadlines EARLY in the process.

There are a number of funds set up for students from financially disadvantaged backgrounds. These include: Financial Assistance for Disadvantaged Health Professions Students (FDHPS), Exceptional Financial Need Scholarships (EFN) and Scholarships for Disadvantaged Students (SDS). Note that FDHPS and EFN require graduates to practice in primary care fields to be eligible.

Students interested in practicing in a primary care field can also apply to the National Health Service Corps, which provides tuition and a monthly stipend in return for service for a specified period of time in an approved, underserved area. For further information, contact:
National Health Service Corps Scholarship Program
Division of Scholarships and Loan Repayments
1010 Wayne Avenue, Suite 240
Silver Spring, MD 20910
1(800) 638-0824
http://nhsc.bhpr.hrsa.gov

The Air Force, Army, Navy and National Guard provide funding for medical school students in the form of full tuition, living allowance and cost of supplies. In return for the financial freedom, students are obligated to serve for the number of years that they receive financial support. See Chapter 7 for more information on working in the Armed Forces. Interested students should contact local recruiters or the following addresses.

Air Force:
Headquarters, U.S. Air Force Recruiting Service
Medical Recruiting Division
Randolph AFB, TX 78150-5421
www.airforce.com

Army:
Headquarters, Department of the Army
ATTN: DASG-PSZ-M
5109 Leesburg Pike
Skyline 6, Room 691
Falls Church, VA 22041-3258
www.goarmy.com

Navy:
Commander, Navy Recruiting Command
4015 Wilson Boulevard
Arlington, VA 22203-1991
www.navy.mil

Minority students may qualify for special programs. The Indian Health Service Scholarship Program will fund Native American and Alaskan students during medical school. For further information, contact:

Indian Health Service Scholarship Program
801 Thompson Avenue, Suite 120
Rockville MD 20852
Phone: (301) 443-6197
www.ihs.gov

The National Association of Medical Minority Educators, Inc. provides scholarships to underrepresented students in the health professions (http://www.namme-hpe.org).

Private organizations also offer many opportunities for educational grants. Students should search the internet or visit the library for these resources. Useful web sites include: www.fastweb.com, www.ed.gov (Department of Education) and www.aamc.org. In addition to providing information on financial planning, AAMC runs a MEDLOANS program. For further information, contact: http://www.aamc.org/students/medloans.

- **Federal Loans**

The Free Application for Federal Student Aid (FAFSA) form is required for federal funds. Students can qualify for Federal Perkins Loan, Federal Stafford or a Federal Direct Loan. The vast majority of medical students carry federal student loans. They offer low interest rates, a grace period before payment is required, and options for deferment, if necessary. Visit http://studentaid.ed.gov or call 1(800) 433-3243.

Low interest rate loans are also available from the federal government for specific groups of students. These include Loans for Disadvantaged Students (exceptional financial need) and Primary Care Loans (for those intending on practicing in a primary care field).

- **Family Gifts or Loans**

Parental or help from other family members may be an option for some students. If you are fortunate, it may come with no interest attached and should be explored before seeking a bank loan. Recent tax law changes provide family members with an advantage also. If given as a gift, the Lifetime Learning Credit allows them to reduce their income tax burden by contributing to your tuition and fees.

- **Personal Bank Loans designed for medical students**

Medical school students have a far easier time qualifying for personal loans with banks as their ability to pay off the loan at the end of training is fairly assured. Some banks have created personal lines of credit for medical students. They offer lower rates of interest, and defer payment of principal until after graduation.

- **Personal Savings or Employment Income**

Personal savings should be the last source of funding. Unexpected needs arise often (car problems, exam preparation course fees, airline travel to another location for an elective), and personal savings may be the only quick access for funds. Students who are considering working while in medical school may be able to do so on a limited basis in the first one to two years, but time constraints won't permit them to work during the last two years of medical school. Even summer work will be difficult as they will be busy preparing for Board Exams or will be in clinical rotations during that time. Employment income is not a viable option for meeting your financial needs during medical school.

Suggested Timeline for the Application Process

College and university students will find the following timeline a useful adjunct in the application process. Use it to get started and keep on target with goals and deadlines. Photocopy the list and tape it to your study desk, then check it off as each one is completed.

Freshman Year:

Obtain a copy of the AAMC's Medical School Admission Requirements and review list of required pre-requisite courses for medical schools

Seek opportunities for involvement in healthcare setting in local hospitals, nursing homes and clinics. Request shadowing opportunities with physicians.

Look for research opportunities

Attend any premedical seminars offered by your college

Sophomore Year:

Start identifying professors and supervisors who can write reference letters

Continue to seek exposure in the medical field

Pick up a book on the MCAT and review it as you cover similar topics in lectures

Look for research opportunities

Junior Year - Fall Semester:

Time to cut down partying

Start studying for the April MCAT (at least 4 months preparation is recommended)

Schedule medical school tours

Review the Medical School Admission Requirements publication thoroughly, noting admission criteria, application deadlines, tuition costs, etc.

Approach 5 suitable referees for letters of recommendation

Review your timetable with Premedical Advisor

Start reading about current medical hot topics and world events

Junior Year - Spring Semester:
Take the April MCAT

Start working on AMCAS essay; write multiple drafts until satisfied, then have it critiqued by an objective person, such as your English professor or premedical advisor

Finalize research on medical schools, complete all tours, and compile your final list

Ensure that MCAT scores, recommendation letters, transcript and personal statement find their way to the appropriate offices

Fill out AMCAS application (first submissions accepted June 1)

Obtain application materials from non-AMCAS schools and submit applications at earliest allowed date

Apply for Early Decision Program, if interested

Summer before Senior Year:
Write August MCAT if previous marks were not satisfactory

Pick up a book on medical ethics

Submit secondary applications

Senior Year - Fall Semester:
Call to confirm that your applications are complete

Start practicing mock interviews. Get advice from medical students - the calls will start coming in soon

Research the medical schools of your choice in depth. Become familiar with the curriculum and philosophy of the school

Continue expanding your knowledge of recent world events and medical news

Look into financial aid resources such as FAFSA for federal financial aid, state government programs and medical school financial aid offices

Early Decision Programs will advise you of your application status. If unsuccessful, submit your application to AMCAS as soon as possible

Interviews take place between September to March

Spring semester:

Contact schools that have wait-listed you, and reiterate your interest in their institution

Consider sending additional letters of recommendation to wait-listed schools

Write thank you letters to interviewers and referees

After receiving letter of acceptance, start looking for accommodation

Summer before medical school:

If accepted to multiple medical schools, decide on your final choice and withdraw from other schools by May

Confirm financial arrangements

Take a well-deserved vacation

Welcome to the beginning of an exciting journey!

Final Thoughts:

Before filling out the application forms, do the necessary groundwork of researching selection criteria and strengths of individual medical schools to make the application process flow smoothly for you. Match your own strengths and interests with those sought by the schools to increase your chances of acceptance. Take full advantage of the financial aid resources available to you as a medical student to pay for your education, particularly when free money is being offered by the government and your school. Lastly, set a timeline for yourself or use the one provided in the chapter to keep yourself on track during the college years. You will need it to get a head-start on three of the most important parts of the application: letters of recommendation, personal statement, and the MCAT.

Chapter 5: Preparing your Application

"He who does not tire, tires adversity."
-Anonymous

By now, you have researched the medical field, attained meaningful exposure to patients, and decided that medicine is the right path for you. By following the CARE mantra, you have worked to maximize your chances of admission. Any medical school would be fortunate to be graced with your presence. But how can you get the word out that you are available? Fortunately, medical schools will give you the chance to showcase your highest potential on the application. They want a motivated, enthusiastic and bright student as much as you want to become a doctor. Medical school students are notorious for having a perfectionist streak in them, and there is no better time to put it to use than in the applications process. Fulfilling all the necessary elements of the application takes months of organization and attention to detail. You have already completed half the task by achieving competitive grades, and getting relevant work and extracurricular experience. Your goals now are to obtain outstanding letters of recommendation, write a winning personal statement, and take the MCAT. With a little bit of guidance, preparing your application doesn't have to be a daunting experience. We will cover the essentials elements of the application in this chapter.

Strategies for Strong Letters of Recommendation

There are many hurdles to cross on the path to being accepted to medical school, and obtaining letters of recommendation is one of the major ones. The process is very unsettling as this is one area where you may feel a lack of control. After all, you will be relying on the good opinions of others to help you enter medical school. But don't get confused between the perception of lack of control and reality. The best letters of recommendation are the ones that you will direct from the beginning.

Medical schools usually request three or more confidential letters of recommendation during the applications process. They will specify the types of letters required, such as a composite letter from a premedical committee at your university, or individual letters from professors or clinicians. It is important to pay attention to their specifications, otherwise your application will be considered incomplete.

If there is a pre-medical or Health Sciences Advisory Committee at your college, it is a good idea to ask for a composite letter of recommendation. Medical schools are familiar with the colleges that offer this option to students, and may wonder why the candidate chose to apply independently if a composite letter isn't submitted. They may wonder if there is a serious concern about your application if you chose not to get the support of the Advisory Committee, such as previous disciplinary action.

The composite letter will address the following issues: major, grades, honors and achievements, rank in class, personal characteristics as described from letters of recommendation submitted to the Committee, inspiration for pursuing medicine as drawn from your personal statement, extracurricular involvement, exposure to medicine, and any previous reprimands by the College. The Committee will ask you to choose between an open and closed file, and reports this decision on the composite letter. If open, it allows you access to all the recommendation letters. While the idea is appealing, it is better to opt for a closed file to avoid giving the impression that you have influenced its contents.

Regardless of whether a composite letter or individual letters of recommendation are required, the best groundwork that you can lay for a strong recommendation is to allow the referee to know you over an extended period of time. This necessitates that you start thinking about the best people to approach as early as possible. Identify the different referees that you will need, for example, professor, physician, pre-medical advisor or employer. One of the best ways is to look at the secondary applications on file at the premed office, search medical school websites, or call and ask the medical school. Try to choose at least 5 people from different fields. For example, two Science professors, one non-Science professor, one physician, one employer and one volunteer supervisor. Remember that the medical school needs to see you as a multi-dimensional candidate.

What does this mean for someone in an Organic Chemistry class that has 300 other students and limited personal interaction with the professor? The Sciences classes will necessarily require more work due to their larger sizes. The most important first step is to make your presence known. Sitting in the front row might make your face recognizable, but it falls short of the mark. Start by asking occasional questions after class. Always introduce yourself until the professor learns your name. Use the tutorial hours on a consistent basis as an opportunity to have longer discussions. This necessitates that you bring interesting questions or topics for discussion. The professor should sense that you have a genuine interest in learning, and that you take initiative in your own education. Try to take more than one course with this professor, thereby allowing the advantage of time as you develop a student-teacher relationship. One of the best ways to establish yourself as a memorable student is to seek an honors project with a professor that you enjoy working with, or take on a summer or part-time research job. Bear in mind that recommendation letters from graduate teaching assistants do not add any strength to your application, unless co-signed by a professor.

Additional letters of reference, such as from a physician who has seen your compassionate side with patients, can also speak volumes about your potential. Once you have targeted the people that you feel would make suitable referees, don't wait until the last minute before the letters are due to approach them. Give them at least two months notice, and they will appreciate the gesture. Professors are often deluged with requests one month prior to the due date, and it is your responsibility to make the process as easy for them as possible.

Second career students who left college many years ago will have to provide the same types of letters as an undergraduate student, but are at a disadvantage due to the time gap. While contacting old professors might be an option, chances are that they may not remember you well enough to write a glowing letter of recommendation. Check with the medical school to see if letters from supervisors or physicians will be accepted in lieu. Also consider taking a few courses to gain contacts with Science professors while brushing up on the required undergraduate subjects.

Requesting a Letter of Recommendation

There is an art to the presentation when approaching potential referees. Start preparing your materials two weeks in advance of the meeting. The following points will guide you in the process:

- **Schedule a suitable time to meet to discuss your interest in medicine**
  Even if the referee is aware of your desire to become a doctor, give a lot of importance to this meeting. Let them know that their opinion of your ability to become a physician is important to you. Speak with confidence. Explain the reasons that you are choosing medicine for a career, and your activities to date that have helped to solidify your decision, such as hospital work experience. Then explicitly ask if they feel that you have the qualities to become a physician. (If they appear the slightest bit hesitant, this is not the right person to solicit for a letter. Thank them for their time, and move on to the next person on your list).

- **Request a strong letter of recommendation**
  Once they have expressed their (hopefully) glowing endorsement of you as a future doctor, ask if they feel they have the time and inclination to write a strong letter of reference on your behalf. Do they feel that they know enough about you as a person to recommend you? For a person who may not have written many medical school recommendations in the past, such as a non-Science professor, you may wish to briefly elaborate on the criteria that medical schools look for, and the part that recommendation letters play in the process.

There is no lack of stories about the less than stellar recommendations that professors occasionally write. A friend requested a letter from a professor, but didn't receive any invitations for an interview that year. To try to determine why, he approached each of his referees for a copy of the letter. In disbelief, he realized that this professor had written a short letter to the effect that the student had attended his class, obtained an A, and would likely make a suitable candidate based on his academic performance, but he had limited knowledge about the student's personal attributes otherwise.

- **Provide additional information for assistance**
  Keep a package with the following documents on hand to give to your referee once they have agreed:
  1) A letter addressed by name, thanking them for taking the time to act as your referee. In the letter, include the capacity in which you knew

them. For example, for a Chemistry professor, mention the classes that you took with him, grades received, as well as any additional work undertaken, such as a project for extra credit. For an employer, write about the job responsibilities that you held under their supervision, and how it helped you develop into a more compassionate/dedicated/broad-minded individual (as appropriate).

2) An updated resume that outlines all your accomplishments, research and clinical work, extracurricular activities, awards and volunteer experiences.

3) A brief summary of personal characteristics that medical schools desire, such as integrity, dedication, cognitive and critical thinking abilities, commitment to lifelong learning, empathy, proficient communication and interpersonal skills, and maturity.

4) A copy of your personal essay

5) Academic transcript (if it's impressive)

6) Copies of any journal articles or publications that lists you as a researcher

7) Addressed, stamped envelope for mailing the recommendation letter to the appropriate office

8) A self-addressed, stamped postcard to be dropped in the mail at the same time that the recommendation letter is mailed out. This will be to inform you that the letter has been sent. This way, you won't become known as that 'annoying student' who keeps calling the office to check on the status of the letter.

- **Explain the contents of the package as you hand it to the referee**

- **Ask if you can provide any further information**

- **Request that the referee contact you should he or she later experience any reservations about you as a medical school applicant.**
  Explain that doubt on their part may mean that you need to re-evaluate your own suitability for a career in medicine.

- **Lastly, relax.**
  You have done all you could to ensure that a compelling letter of recommendation will be written. You also provided multiple safety checks along the way to avoid the possibility of a lukewarm or damaging letter: you assessed the referee's enthusiasm by asking for verbal feed

back on your career choice, asked if they felt comfortable writing a strong letter of recommendation, and added a caveat at the end of contacting you if they changed their minds. Now that you have expertly dealt with the reference letters, it's time to bring out the writer in you as you compose a personal essay.

Tips for Writing an Effective Personal Statement

Each medical school receives hundreds of applications each year. Prestigious medical schools receive up to a few thousand. There is little variation among the academic qualifications of candidates. Candidates need an opportunity to stand out from the crowd, and the personal statement is the ideal forum. A well written essay can also help to balance out any minor academic deficiencies.

The official guidelines instruct students to consider the following questions when composing the essay: why they have chosen the field of medicine, motivation for learning more about medicine, individual challenges faced during their educational career, comments on any significant discrepancies in their academic record, in addition to any other information students would like the Admissions Committee to know. The amount of space allocated for the statement is 5300 characters, or one typewritten page.

Students tend to underestimate the importance of this part of the application. The personal statement is the first opportunity for the Admissions Committee to assess your personality, motivations, communication skills, and maturity. The second written opportunity will come with the secondary application, when the schools will ask for answers to specific questions, such as your interest in their school. In the personal statement, the Admissions Committee is looking for a reason to invite you for a personal interview, and your objective is to provide that reason on a silver platter in the form of a persuasive autobiographical statement. The Committee wants to know whether you have the desire to make a meaningful contribution to society.

There are many different approaches to writing a winning essay, but they all share some common elements. One of the most important is to show evidence of clarity of purpose. The fundamental question that needs to be answered is "Why have you chosen medicine?" The theme of the essay should be geared at providing a clear, explicit answer. Essays that merely hint at the reasons won't be considered strong enough. The Committee members need to know that you have asked and answered this question in your own mind, and can explain your reasons with confidence. They will use the essay as a basis for questions during the medical school interview.

Provide evidence of knowledge about the medical field. While the Admissions Committee won't expect you to know much about the technical aspects of medicine, you will be expected to have an insight on the duties of a doctor and the unique relationship that exists between doctor and patient. Your words will be convincing if the insight has been a result of knowledge gained firsthand in the medical field, either as a volunteer, researcher or employee. The extent to which you attempted to gain in-depth knowledge about the medical field will also be noted.

Demonstrate qualities of compassion, maturity, independent thinking and leadership skills through your actions rather than words. For example, consider a student who starts as a volunteer and then works her way up to the position of a crisis counselor over a period of four years, while simultaneously enrolled as a fulltime college student. She has clearly demonstrated commitment and caring through her dedication. Notice that this approach is far more effective than stating 'I feel that I have compassion for others'.

Some may advise that your essay not contain information that has been included elsewhere in the AMCAS application, such as awards or research experience. Instead, they argue, it should focus on creating a portrait of your personality. However, there are many schools that will ask questions based on the personal statement during the interview. This makes it imperative that the personal statement stand as its own testament to your abilities and potential. Attempting to describe personal characteristics without evidence of the work that you have put into developing yourself into an accomplished and well-rounded individual will give a hollow effect to the essay. It is not necessary to go into minute details of all your accomplishments and extracurricular activities, but do include unique life experiences and the most important aspects of your clinical work, research experience and awards that highlight educational or humanitarian efforts.

Students often use a story as a key point in the personal statement. Use experiences from your life to create an engaging and personal essay by using it as an illustration of a larger point. Use the story to further your theme, but don't allow the essay to end without emphasizing how it relates to you as a future doctor. Keeping these tips in mind, plan an outline of your essay prior to starting the first draft. The most effective essays start with an interesting opening, such as a relevant quote, question or an interesting event in your life. Avoid boring openings such as "I was born in…" or "I want to go to medical school because…" The first two paragraphs of the essay should make the thesis clear. This will be the glue that holds your essay together. The body of the essay comes next, and this is the place to elaborate on your thesis, using examples from your life. If discussing the qualities that make a good doctor, show how you have attempted to develop those qualities in yourself. Make the connection between your passions and activities. Include reflection on important activities that you have undertaken. For example, a candidate who has volunteered in an underprivileged community might reflect on the insight gained on the relationship between health and poverty. Lastly, conclude with reference back to the thesis of the essay. Don't summarize your paragraphs, as this is a short essay. Strive for a memorable closing. Your goal is to convince the Admissions Committee that you would be an asset to the medical profession and your future patients.

The technical qualities of the essay are just as important as the content. Spelling or grammatical mistakes show lack of attention to detail. Admissions Committees fully expect that you have taken the utmost care in preparing your application. Careless mistakes distract attention from the importance of your words. The first draft of any piece of work is rarely satisfactory. Your essay will benefit from several re-writes to find the right words. Spend sufficient time composing the statement until you are satisfied. Set it aside for a few days, then return to it with a fresh point of view. After you have produced a polished draft, obtain critiques from people whose opinion you trust. Choose someone familiar with the medical field, as well as someone whose strength lies in the art of composition, such as your English professor. The latter, particularly, will be able to help with essays that lack an organizing theme.

Ask the following questions during the revision process:
1) Does the essay contain all the key information that you want to convey to the Admissions Committee?
2) Does it demonstrate your strength of character and motivation?
3) Does it answer why you have chosen medicine as a career?
4) Does it have a strong opening and ending? Is it memorable?
5) Is it detailed enough to sustain interest? Does it avoid generalities?
6) Is the thesis clear?
7) Are there examples or anecdotes from your own life?
8) Does your statement reflect a person with a balanced self-image?

A helpful resource for writing personal statements is *Medical School Admissions: The Insider's Guide*. It contains 50 sample personal statements of medical school students from across the United States. Use it for inspiration, but speak in your own voice.

The following example of a well-written essay is provided for guidance. The author manages to convey a clear motivation for applying to medical school. His opening quote and closing sentence provide the theme to the essay, and allow him to describe his background and achievements in its context. The student's sincerity and sense of purpose are its most striking features. Most importantly, he provides the necessary scholastic and clinical achievements that would allow the Admissions Committee to consider him as a serious candidate.

Sample Personal Statement

It was one of the most notable physicians of our century, Sir William Osler, who said: "To have striven, to have made the effort, to have been true to certain ideals - this alone is worth the struggle."

This statement has helped to define the role of a dedicated physician for me. As a nurse's aide in the Department of Medicine at Babylon Hospital, I was fortunate to be a part of the lives of many memorable patients. Their struggles, whether it was learning to walk again after a stroke, or recuperating from heart surgery, were a daily lesson to me on the power of the human spirit to recover. I was struck by the ability of physicians to guide their patients through the stages of grief and anger over an illness, and yet be able to simultaneously instill hope for the future. This isn't just a testament to the difference that modern medicine can make in a person's life, but also to a doctor's ability to provide the compassionate care that leads to a unique trusting relationship between doctor and patient.

It was Dr. A, in particular, who first captured my attention. He is a neurologist, but I suspect that he is more than that to his patients. I would study him at the bedside with interest as he would take out a myriad of metallic instruments such as a tendon hammer, ophthalmoscope and a pin to test eyes, knees and feet. It was his manner, though, that held my interest. From inquiring about the patient's grandchild to sitting by the bed listening with rapt attention as the patient described his worries, he made it clear that he would see this patient through his ordeal of ill health. I doubt that any patient ever felt the glare of the ophthalmoscope light, or the prick of the pin when in the company of a physician who showed such obvious thoughtfulness.

I often tried to imagine myself as that doctor, and would practice by listening to my patients. I learnt about their lives, fears and hopes. I listened some more, and I soon discovered that these patients had become my greatest teachers. They inspired me to try to help them in a capacity greater than I could fulfill as a nurse's aide, and this became my challenge.

Three years ago, I committed myself to an undergraduate sciences program at University A, and began my journey. I found myself enjoying, and even excelling, in the curriculum. This is because the source of my inspiration, my patients, never lay far from me, as I continued to work as a full-time nurse's aide while attending University. This past year, I was privileged to work with Dr. B in his chemistry lab as part of an honors project. The research question centered on the magnetic properties and photochromism of compounds containing mercury. Our findings have been recently submitted for publication to Journal C.

During the summers between the undergraduate years, I volunteered at an inner city clinic and realized the large impact that medical professionals can make in the lives of the disadvantaged. With the support of Dr. D, I organized a youth clinic, held once a week, which educated teenagers about the prevalence of HIV and Hepatitis B. We were successful in obtaining a grant for our work from organization E, and used the funds to vaccinate over two hundred youths against Hepatitis B.

As little as three years ago, I hadn't realized that such a remarkable education lay ahead of me. Now, my experiences in the medical field have solidified my desire to use the best medical knowledge and interpersonal skills possible for the betterment of lives threatened by disease. I've had a chance to test myself academically as well as clinically, and found that Dr. William Osler was right. I can only look forward to the next part of my life where, if given the opportunity, I will continue to strive as a doctor to make one life a little better at a time. That is all that is needed to create a real lasting change, and that alone *is* worth the struggle.

Medical College Admissions Test

The MCAT is the first in the series of multiple standardized tests that a physician is required to take. This exam plays a key role in creating a favorable first impression on the Admissions Committee. While grades and letters of recommendation do provide important information about the applicant, it is the MCAT that levels the playing field for all candidates. The MCAT has no regard for the undergraduate institution you attended, or the grades you received in university.

Virtually all medical schools in the United States require the MCAT as part of the admissions application. The role that the MCAT plays varies from one medical school to another. Some use it as screening criteria. For example, only candidates with a minimum score specified by the school will be eligible to apply. All candidates who meet the criteria would be evaluated by the Admissions Committee, but the final weight of the MCAT in the application process might only be 25% beyond screening. Most schools, however, place a heavy emphasis on the MCAT, giving it as much as 50% weight in the final decision.

The good news about the MCAT is that you will have covered the courses required for the exam as part of the pre-requisites for medical school. The material will already seem familiar as you begin studying. Unless you have a long-term photographic memory though, do not rely on prior knowledge alone. The MCAT requires active preparation started at least four months ahead of the exam for the average candidate. Getting a good score on this exam is not an easy feat. While all professional entrance exams are challenging, the MCAT requires an enormous amount of scientific knowledge as well as good written communication skills. It is likely the longest exam you will have written so far in college, but get used to it. The average Medical Board Exam is just as long, and you will be required to write at least three of these to be licensed as a doctor.

Students often wonder about the best time to write the MCAT. It is offered twice a year, in April and August. Both dates have their advantages and disadvantages, and you will need to weigh them carefully when making your decision. The majority of medical school candidates write the MCAT in April of the application year. In case they don't perform as well as anticipated, they have the option of re-writing it in August and still being on time for medical school admission at most institutions for the following year. However, writing the MCAT in August does mean that medical schools have to wait until October to receive the score, thereby delaying the decision to offer interviews until later in the admissions process.

The April exam date is the only option if participating in the Early Decision Program. In addition, writing it in April means that you can focus on preparing the application during the summer instead of studying for the exam. Since the results will be out by June, it can also help you decide on which schools to apply to, depending on how well you did.

Writing the exam in April has disadvantages also. Most colleges hold their final exams in April, so you will be studying for college courses as well as the MCAT at the same time. However, if most of your courses are Biochemistry, Organic and Inorganic Chemistry and Biology, there will be significant overlap of material. In this case, studying simultaneously might prove easier.

There is an extensive amount of material to cover for the MCAT- first year Physics, Inorganic Chemistry, Organic Chemistry, Biology as well as English language skills, such as verbal reasoning and essay writing. The Physical Sciences, Biological Sciences and Verbal Reasoning sections of the MCAT are graded on a scale of 1-15. Attaining a 15 would put a student in the 99.9 percentile, and is rare. A general guideline is that a score of 10 and higher is fairly competitive. A score less than 7 in any section indicates an area requiring considerable improvement. It is important to do well in all sections. A score of 13 in Physical Sciences and 7 in Biological Sciences won't make a favorable impression. The actual number of questions in each section has changed over the years, but the basic format of a passage followed by questions remains the same. There are also independent questions within each section. The exam allows 85 minutes for the Verbal Reasoning Section, 100 minutes for Biological Sciences, 60 minutes for two written essays, and 100 minutes for Physical Sciences.

The writing sample section is divided into two parts. Two essays need to be written over an hour, and each one is strictly limited to thirty minutes each. This means that you cannot use time left over from the first essay to finish the second. The exam will present a broad statement for discussion, such as 'Understanding history leads to a better understanding of the present'. The examinee's task is to explain the statement, and prepare a discussion based on the specific questions following the statement. The essay portions are scored on a letter system, ranging between J (lowest) to T (highest).

Many candidates do not pay much attention to the verbal reasoning or writing skills portion of the exam, but these are invariably the two sections where Science students do the most poorly. A number of preparation books are available for guidance, and it is strongly recommended that candidates use them to assess the scope of the exam. Questions on the MCAT have a specific focus, often different from the types of exam questions you faced in college science exams, so it is important understand the objectives of the exam prior to taking it for the first time. Students can choose to write the MCAT more than once if they are dissatisfied with their scores. However, scores from all attempts will be reported to medical schools, and the school's individual policies determine how they utilize the marks. Some may only consider the best effort, while others may average out scores from multiple attempts.

Preparation courses are available from companies such as Kaplan. These courses are run as classes, with opportunities for multiple practice exams. They aren't necessary for achieving high scores on the MCAT if you are committed to studying on a regular basis. Students who might find them useful are those who benefit from instructor support in a classroom environment.

Previous MCAT questions are available through the AAMC. There are also many test books available in bookstores that attempt to simulate the type of questions tested on the actual exam. It is worthwhile to obtain a copy of at least one full-length MCAT from AAMC to simulate an actual exam. Take this practice test under the same standardized conditions as the real MCAT. Allot specified times for each section, and take breaks only as allowed on the real test. Using the scoring tables at the end of the test, you will have a good idea of your abilities at the present level of preparation.

The MCAT can prove to be a lesson in stamina, as it requires 7 hours to complete it. I witnessed a number of students with frazzled nerves and even tears during the halfway mark on my exam day. Unfortunately, the only magic pill for stress during the MCAT is diligent preparation.

Testing and Registration

Many schools will not accept MCAT scores that are more than two or three years old. The Medical School Admissions Requirements provides the MCAT requirements of different schools. This information is also readily available on the websites of individual schools. More than 600 test centre sites are available in North America, including Guam, Puerto Rico and the Virgin Islands. There are thirteen international test sites. The exam is offered in April and August of each year. View the official MCAT website at: www.aamc.org/students/mcat/registration.htm

For questions about registration and testing, contact:
MCAT Program Office
P.O. Box 4056
Iowa City, IA 52243
(319) 337-1357
mcat_reg@act.org

Final Thoughts:

Obtaining letters of recommendation, composing a personal statement, and writing the MCAT are the most challenging parts of the application process for medical school. These components of the evaluation process can help you to stand out as a candidate when approached thoughtfully, so give your undivided attention to them. If the applications process seems far too demanding, wait until you are a doctor! Be forewarned that long hours and hard work await you at the finish line. It requires a passion to become a physician, and a personality that is willing to push itself harder with every new challenge. This trait will be important for the final step before you gain entry into the medical world - the personal interview.

Chapter 6: Medical School Interviews

"If at first you do succeed, try not to look too surprised."
-Anonymous

The medical school interview process is unlike any other that you'll ever experience. At a typical job interview, you would be out to sell a set of skills that directly affected the profit margin of the employer. However, at this interview, your goal is to convince a panel of your future ability to contribute to society. Your potential as an individual who will have to make grave decisions as a medical doctor will be judged.

The truth is that the thrill of being invited for an interview is second only to the elation of receiving the letter of acceptance into medical school. An invitation to the school to meet members of the Admissions Committee is a significant accomplishment. It means that your application has been reviewed and found to be competitive. Now, the Committee members are interested in a personal meeting to identify traits and characteristics that will convince them of your ability to succeed in the medical field. Tough questions will be asked in a short amount of time to make a decision about your suitability. It is not only an interview for school admission, but also of suitability for a demanding career.

Acing the Interviews

The goal of the Admissions Committee is to find future physicians who are not only intelligent, but possess the necessary qualities to provide compassionate and humane care to patients. Whereas medical knowledge can be easily taught during the years spent in medical school and residency, the elusive quality of character cannot. Therefore, schools rely on the interview process to select applicants who can provide that unique combination of commitment and intellectual ability needed in the medical field.

Exceptional candidates who have already displayed their potential through their grades, MCAT scores, personal statement and recommendation letters will find that the interview can add the final stamp of approval. Provided that the applicant is amiable, empathetic, possesses proficient interpersonal skills, and doesn't appear to harbor any glaring deficiencies in character, the interview process is unlikely to damage the rest of his application. However, the interview should never be treated as a mere formality. Even candidates who look like stars on paper can turn out to be poor interviewees. An inability to communicate adequately, or a show of insincerity, will always result in rejection.

Candidates who are in the grey zone for acceptance academically can greatly enhance their chances through a successful interview. Certain schools rank the interview as being equally as important as grades and MCAT scores. Again, this demonstrates the importance that schools place on finding genuine, well-balanced candidates to enter medical school.

Every little effort counts at this stage. Even though your probability of gaining medical school acceptance has greatly increased by being invited for an interview, the battle isn't over. So far, the work of convincing the Committee has taken place from a distance. Each word in your application and personal statement was carefully weighed before being allowed to pass under the Committee's scrutinizing eyes. But now, the moment of truth has arrived. It is your turn to stand as proof of the information that you provided in your application. It is no longer a case of 'tell me', but 'show me'. Your mission is to convince them that you not only deserve to be a part of the school, but that the medical profession is in dire need of an intelligent and considerate future doctor such as yourself.

Does it sound like an impossible task? It did to me at the time. Most good doctors are, in fact, a modest lot. Speaking highly of oneself can be a forced effort. For the medical school interview, however, consider it your responsibility to speak confidently about your abilities. The best way to overcome any discomfort about doing so is to keep practicing with another person until you feel at ease with it.

The interview day usually starts with an orientation session. Candidates receive a copy of their interviewer's names and interview times. There will be a brief presentation on the school, followed by a discussion of the scheduled events. This usually involves a tour of the lecture halls and lab facilities of the medical school. While each school differs in their approach, an interview usually lasts between twenty minutes to one hour. There might be individual interviews with one or more members of the Committee, or panel interviews. Committee members are made up of Science professors, clinical faculty, members of the community and, occasionally, medical students. Some medical schools provide the interviewers with your entire file in advance, while others may provide only portions of your application, such as the personal statement. You may want to contact the medical school before your interview date to find out its procedures.

You will meet many different types of medical school hopefuls during the interview process. The anxiety level in the waiting area is usually quite high, and all personality types are revealed in this emotional state. You will undoubtedly encounter Mr. I-was-born-to-do-medicine, and Ms. You-might-as-well-go-home-because-I'm-better and even some I'm-too-good-for-this-dump mentalities. Pay no attention to them, as these are strategies to allay their own nervousness. Use your time wisely and discuss any questions you might have with the medical students who conduct the tours. They don't have an input in the admissions game, so feel free to ask questions that medical students are privy to, such as the competitive nature of students in the school, weaknesses in the program, etc.

Unlike the MCAT, which provides a standardized basis for comparison of students, the interview format will vary greatly between interviewers. There are standard questions that are virtually guaranteed at every interview, such as 'Tell me why you are choosing medicine'. The content of the interview is usually left to the discretion of the person conducting it, and this has led to some absurd questions as well, such as 'What do you know about mitochondrial DNA?'

Count on at least one or more odd questions during the interviews. They will rarely make a real difference in the final assessment. The good news is that there are specific actions that can be taken to enhance the chances of success on the interview day. The first is becoming familiar with the common types of questions that are asked, and the second is learning the secrets to becoming the ideal interviewee.

Common Interview Themes

There is no shortage of information that can be studied in preparation for the interview, so the key is to identify the common themes. Preparation should start weeks to months earlier, by keeping updated on recent medical news, present concerns about the healthcare system, and world events. These topics may not even come up in all settings, but it is better to be prepared in case your interviewer wants to be assured that you do manage to keep up with life outside of school.

Information on current political medical issues can be found in the American Medical Association News or AMA website (http://www.ama-assn.org). For your own interest, you may want to gain familiarity with respected medical journals such as the New England Journal of Medicine. Databases such as MEDLINE and PubMed, sponsored by the National Library of Medicine and the National Institutes of Health, are also used by students, residents and physicians to gain information on clinical and research information. The content matter of scientific journals is highly unlikely to come up in the interview though, so do not spend too much time on these as part of your preparation.

The common topics for questions in the interview tend to be:
1. Personal questions - background, motivations, aspirations, influences, strengths and weaknesses
2. Healthcare issues
3. Medical Ethics
4. Challenges in the medical profession
5. Current events

The most popular questions based on these topics have been included with sample answers at the end of this chapter.

Interviewers do not expect that you will have all the answers, but they will note how you choose to answer. They will be looking for evidence of objectivity in your responses. They realize that the interview is a stressful experience for students. They don't expect the perfect answer to every question, as this entity doesn't exist. They do, however, hope to find genuineness and sincerity in your responses.

The majority of interviewers ask reasonable questions, but some inquiries into your life might be controversial, and even outrageous. Interviewers have been known to ask them to assess your ability to handle an anxiety-provoking situation. Stress interviews are designed to make you feel intimidated. The proverbial examples are the student being asked to open a window that has been nailed shut, or sit on a broken chair. While these cases are cited frequently in interview horror stories, I have yet to hear real cases of them. However, situations that have come up with my own interviews and those of colleagues include: the interviewer appearing bored throughout the interview by looking out the window or at his watch, reading the newspaper as you answer his questions, scoffing at your answer, commenting to a co-interviewer that your responses sound naïve, challenging your personal beliefs about religion, politics or sexuality, and inquiring into your personal contraceptive choices. You get the idea.

An interviewee who perceives these questions as a personal attack is bound to either reply with sarcasm or withdraw emotionally from the interview. The best approach to answering such questions is to be diplomatic, and to never take it too personally. The interviewer has nothing to gain by offending you, but you have a lot to gain by answering rationally and maturely. Such cases are isolated, and most likely won't be a part of your experience. However, in case the situation does arise, handle it professionally. The interviewer may appear to have the personality of a despot, but don't let the words stick to you and cause aggravation. A pleasant smile and deep breath, followed by a tactful answer will win you points. Applicants are given the opportunity to write an evaluation of the interview process and the interviewers afterwards. If you feel that the interviewer was intentionally malicious, you can address it on the evaluation, or ask to speak to another Committee member about your experience.

Non-traditional and older students tend to do well in interviews, likely because they have a broader perspective and the advantage of life experience. However, anyone can do well if they are able to anticipate most of the questions and put in the effort and time into practicing at every opportunity.

Watch yourself in the mirror as you practice. Do you look confident? Recruit friends and family to conduct mock interviews. Would they want you to be their doctor based on your answers? Pay attention to your habits. Do you fiddle with your hands as you answer, bite your lip, or look at the wall instead of the interviewer? Try to overcome these distracting habits through regular practice. The same applies to speech mannerisms. You wouldn't want your doctor to use 'umms' liberally in his sentences as he speaks to you. It reflects hesitation and doubt, so try not to do the same.

Becoming the Ideal Interviewee

The key to becoming the ideal interviewee is to follow some basic, common-sense guidelines for preparation, personal conduct, and use specific interview strategies.

As the interview day approaches, organize yourself by going through the following:

1. Decide on your interview attire. Medical school candidates tend to wear conservative attire, usually in navy, grey or black. Polish shoes.
2. Review your autobiographical data, AMCAS application, resume, and secondary applications. The bulk of the interview will be focused on you, so it is important that you know the details of your application well. If you have research experience, be able to speak fluently about the objectives, methodology, results and implications of the data, even if the research was done years ago.
3. Make a list of the major points that you want the Admissions Committee to know about you. Aim to incorporate all these items during the interview and relate these strengths to your potential as a future doctor.
4. Review information about the school. The interviewers will want to know why you have chosen to apply there. Review the information provided in the catalog, website, and speak to any contacts at the school.
5. Prepare three to five questions for the interviewer. It demonstrates interest on your end, and will also allow you to find out information beyond those provided in the official publications.
6. Keep copies of personal statement, AMCAS profile, secondary application, and resume in your bag. Use them for your own review or in case the school has misplaced some of the information. (It does happen).
7. If you have any relevant materials that enhance your application, such as copies of your published article, take it along. Offer to show it to the interviewer.
8. Peruse recent newspapers and watch news reports for current events.
9. Review a book on biomedical ethics
10. Keep aside thank-you cards for mailing to the interviewer after the interview.

Never exaggerate your skills or credentials. Your integrity will be irreversibly damaged if the interviewer is also knowledgeable in the area and realizes that you have inflated your abilities, or worse, been dishonest. For example, a university colleague had listed fluency in Spanish on her application, but fell short of the mark when the interviewer decided to conduct the entire interview in Spanish!

Review the following tips for the interview day:

- Arrive fifteen minutes early for the interview.
- Be pleasant, make lots of eye contact, and smile often.
- Have a firm handshake.
- Speak courteously to all staff - especially secretaries. They are your allies in the applications process as all your phone calls about application status will be handled by them.
- Listen to the interviewer's questions carefully, and don't interrupt them.
- Most questions will be open-ended. Decide ahead of time how you will handle these, as most candidates tend to keep talking to fill in dead space out of nervousness.
- If you don't understand a question, ask for clarification.
- Always be direct and honest in your answers. Interviewers are skilled at picking out insincere applicants.
- Be specific. Illustrate with examples. Overly vague answers and generalizations are never convincing.
- Pay attention to your seating position. Sitting at the edge of the seat indicates nervousness. Folded arms and crossed legs appear that you are 'closed' off to the interviewer.
- Speak confidently and at a regular pace - anxiety tends to speed up speech
- Plan to be active during the interview. You are not there just to answer their questions. Use all opportunities to provide more information about your superb qualifications for medical school.
- Do take your time with more difficult questions. Articulate before you speak.
- Elaborate on questions, even for yes and no answers. Allow the interviewer to gain insight into your thinking process.
- Don't try to fabricate answers to questions. Answering 'I don't know' is perfectly acceptable. Depending on the question, you can state that you can find out the answer and get back to the interviewer at a later time. A word of caution: do not overuse this strategy. It seems appropriate to use it only once during an interview.
- Don't use notes during the interview. It speaks of poor preparation and lack of confidence.
- Be vibrant. Avoid passive, rehearsed answers.
- Avoid disparaging remarks about any person or life situation.
- Avoid controversial topics.

- Don't ask tactless questions such as 'I heard about the scandal with that professor. What happened with that?'
- Relax! Most interviews are quite enjoyable. You may end up learning a lot about yourself.

During my interview experiences, I saw a candidate being asked to leave after he got into an argument with an interviewer. Another walked out halfway through her interview as she didn't like the nature of questions being asked. Following medical school, I've had the chance to interview with numerous hospitals for internship as well as residency positions. These were far more relaxed and friendly than the med school interviews, lending truth to the statement that the hardest part about medical school is getting in!

Sample Interview Questions

The following are actual questions that have been asked during medical school interviews. Some are followed by comments that are intended as examples of acceptable answers. Your answer should be based on your own thoughts and experiences. Use the sample answers as a starting point for self-exploration, and for finding your strengths and style. Most interview questions rarely have right or wrong responses, but the candidate should be able to demonstrate an intelligent and considered thought process.

Personal

1. Why do you want to study medicine?

There isn't much variation to the types of answers that can be given here, so state your reasons and support them with the life circumstances that led to applying for medical school. eg. "I made the decision to pursue medicine when I realized that I could combine my interests with my abilities in this field. Even from a young age, I have been drawn to trying to make a difference in the lives of those less fortunate than me. For example, in high school, I started helping out with the physical therapy of a child with cerebral palsy every weekend. Jon was severely handicapped, both physically and mentally. I didn't understand his disease particularly well, but I could see that my presence, as well as those of the other volunteers, comforted him. I continued to work with him for three years, until the complications of his disease led to his death. Later, when I joined university, I started volunteering every week at a nursing home, doing occupational and physical therapy with seniors. I found that I could reconnect to that same sense of purpose that I had shared with Jon. That's when I started thinking about a career in medicine, and began looking into what is required to become a doctor. Since then, I've had the chance to learn more about medicine by shadowing doctors at Hospital X. All these experiences have confirmed at every step that I can make a real difference in people's lives. I've found that medicine offers real relief to those in pain and suffering and I want to be a part of that."

Notice that this answer addresses compassion, empathy, motivation and the student's own efforts to learn more about medicine through a wide range of exposures. She has connected to the deepest reason for seeking to become a doctor, and that is to help elevate the human condition to a higher level. Her chances of admission are above average at this point, and if the remainder of her application is just as strong, she is likely to receive multiple acceptance letters.

2. When did you decide that you wanted to be a doctor?

There is nothing wrong with saying that you've wanted to be one for as long as you can remember, but try to support your lifelong ambition with experiences as an adult that strengthened your conviction to enter medicine.

Be wary of answers that sound as if you still haven't made the decision to be a doctor, and are merely testing the waters to see if you get accepted into medical school. If this is really the case, consider your true aspirations. If you are torn between being a doctor and pursuing a PhD, an MBA or a law degree, there are programs that combine these interests. See Chapter 7 for more information on these programs. If you are interested in another field altogether, you owe it to yourself to discover the right field before joining a rigorous, demanding program that won't meet your needs.

3. What type of medicine do you want to practice?

If you have a good idea about your future practice, then feel free to elaborate. However, a significant number of medical students change their minds during medical school, and it is acceptable to say that you would like to go through clinical rotations before making a final decision. Some medical schools have an interest in training general practice or rural physicians, and if these are your interests as well, let the Committee know.

4. Who have been positive influences in your life?

You're on your own to come up with some names, but elaborate on the qualities that inspired you to choose them. Usually, these influences are past teachers, parents, physicians, etc. How has your life changed because of these influences?

What lessons have they taught you? How will you be a better doctor because of them?

5. Where do you see yourself ten years from now?

This question isn't referring to the type of lifestyle you wish to have. Answer in terms of whether you see yourself as a professor in a medical school, researcher, clinician, etc. There are a number of clinicians who also do research, so any combination of these is acceptable. Do you anticipate working in a large city or within a smaller community? Is there a specific population that you wish to work with, such as underserved minority groups or inner city populations?

6. What three adjectives would you use to describe yourself?

If the following words describe you, use them! These adjectives have been used by medical schools to describe the qualities that they seek in medical school candidates: approachable, balanced, committed, compassionate, creative, dependable, diverse, empathetic, enthusiastic, honest, humanitarian, intellectually curious, mature, motivated, sincere, socially aware, unique. They also look for candidates with integrity, leadership potential and an ability to work well with others.

7. Why should we choose you over another qualified candidate?

Don't be afraid of being asked such a question. It gives you the best chance of convincing the interviewer that you deserve a seat in their medical school. When the Admissions Committee convenes to discuss all candidates, the interviewer's role is to act as your advocate. This question allows you to give the interviewer reasons that he can later use to convince the Admissions Committee of your potential.

Your goal is to sound confident as you prove your suitability over other candidates, not egocentric. There can be a fine line, so pay attention to the way that you phrase your answer. eg. "I recognize that a medical school class will have many talented, intelligent and caring students. I feel that I can add to such a class through my unique qualities also. Some of these are..."

8. What will you do if you don't get accepted into medical school?

The interviewer is hoping to hear that you will either improve your application and apply again, or will consider an allied health care field. They are looking for a dedication to patient care. If your answer tells them that you intend on switching tracks completely to pursue corporate law, it will torpedo your application.

9. How do you handle stress?

Physical activity, such as exercise or sports, music, painting, and turning to your social support systems of family and friends are constructive methods that are encouraged in medical school.

10. What interests do you have?

If you are an accomplished artist or athlete, allow your passion to shine through on this question. Also, diversity makes for an interesting person. Make a list of your interests prior to the interview, and pick the ones that bring out your natural enthusiasm.

11. Describe the most difficult person you ever met.

This is a tricky question, as it is asking you to describe the worst qualities of another individual. Keep in mind that the way you describe others gives a better idea of who you are and how you judge others than the person under question. Focus on the valuable lessons that you learnt from this person rather than the grief and frustration you may have endured. As has been said, our biggest challenges are our best teachers.

12. Why have you applied to our school?

Focus on the aspects of the school that hold meaning for you, such as location, research facilities, history of medical student involvement in community projects, innovative teaching such as a problem-based learning curriculum, early exposure to patients, diverse patient population in the area, and opportunities for electives in other states or countries.

Additional Practice Questions:

12. What are the qualities of a good doctor?
13. What is your greatest strength/weakness?
14. What has been your greatest challenge?
15. What has been your biggest accomplishment?
16. What support systems do you have to help you through medical school?
17. What are you passionate about?
18. What makes you unique?
19. How do you feel about dying patients?
20. When did you decide to become a doctor?
21. Tell me about the research you've done.
22. How will you finance your medical education?

23. Why didn't you choose nursing or social work to help people?
24. What is the last book you read (or movie you saw)? Tell me about it.
25. What did you enjoy most about your undergraduate education?

Healthcare Issues

1. What are pressing healthcare concerns in the United States today?
Take your pick (there are many more):
- 45 million people lacking healthcare coverage in the U.S.
- The rising costs of healthcare and prescription drugs
- 78 million baby boomers will be retiring within a decade - can we afford the rising costs of long-term and chronic care?
- Disparities in access to treatment for rural communities and indigent populations
- Rising costs of educating healthcare workers and shortage of qualified healthcare staff
- Emergence of new diseases: HIV/AIDS in 1982, SARS in 2003
- Protecting patient confidentiality as information becomes more disseminated and readily available
- Increasing obesity rate among adults and children

2. What are world-wide healthcare concerns?
Recent or ongoing concerns:
- Spread of HIV/AIDS in Africa, India, Caribbean, etc
- Emerging communicable diseases such as SARS
- Bioterrorism threats
- Lack of basic necessities: clean water, shelter, freedom, food
- Lack of access to medical centers and treatments

3 What has been the most significant achievement in the medical field in the past century?
Consider the following topics for discussion:
- Controlling disease through vaccinations (from the days of Jenner to present)
- Use of antiseptics to combat infection during surgeries (early 1900's)
- Discovery of penicillin (1920's, but wasn't widely used until 1940's)
- First successful organ transplant (1950's)
- Human Genome Project to identify genes in human DNA (1990's)

Additional Practice Questions:

4. Where do you think medicine is headed in the near future?
5. What are the biggest concerns for doctors in this state?
6. What is the difference between Medicare and Medicaid?
7. How can we improve healthcare in the U.S.?
8. Should we get rid of medical health insurance and adopt a socialized healthcare system?

Medical Ethics

These questions never have right or wrong answers from an ethical point of view, but they often do from a legal perspective. The best approach is to recognize that both sides have valid points, and talk briefly about the pros and cons. Then, if there is no clear answer, it is acceptable to say that you would follow the rules and regulations of the hospital, as well as the laws of the state/country in performing your duty.

To prepare for ethical questions, review a book on biomedical ethics prior to the interview, and note down the main principles: autonomy (patient's right to make own decisions), beneficence (strive to take actions to benefit the patient), non-maleficence (do no harm) and distributive justice (fairness of proposed action). These four principles will help to formulate an intelligent discussion on any ethical issue.

1. If a patient with a terminal illness requested your help with euthanasia, what would you do?
The duty of a physician is first to identify why the patient seeks euthanasia. How have they coped with their condition in the past? Has something changed recently that has altered their perspective on living? Patients with chronic conditions or terminal diseases are very susceptible to depression, and this can lead to suicidal thoughts. Would this patient be helped by interventions to treat depression? What additional support systems can be enlisted - pastoral help, family support, etc.

The law prohibits euthanasia, so your professional obligations to your patient have been pre-determined by the laws of the state. However, by trying to understand the situation better, you may help to alleviate some of the despair, fear and sense of hopelessness that your patient is experiencing.

2. You have been seeing a 3 year old child in your clinic for the past year, and she has come in twice in the past 6 months with atypical bruises. Her parents are professors at a prestigious university, and state that she received the bruises at day-

care. You are concerned about child abuse. What would you do?

Abuse occurs at all socio-economic levels. Doctors are required by law to report any suspicion about child abuse to law enforcement and child protection authorities.

Additional Practice Questions:

3. If one patient needed a liver transplant due to chronic alcohol abuse, and another needed it because of hepatitis C which he acquired from a blood transfusion, who should get that transplant?
4. If a child needed a bone marrow transplant within the next month in order to survive, but his parents wanted to try scientifically unproven alternative therapies first, what would you advise?
5. What are your feelings about abortion? Would you perform it on a patient who would otherwise die?
6. Should organs be distributed based on age, health or ability to pay?

Challenges in the Medical Profession

1.   How will you balance your personal life with your career?

Women tend to get these types of questions far more often than men. Some interviewers might even ask if you intend on becoming pregnant in the near future. Though such questions are considered 'illegal' and are offensive to many, answer calmly. In a medical practice, there will be situations when patients will ask highly personal questions. Therefore, treat these interview questions as training grounds for when an inquisitive patient will ask you more than you are willing to tell.

One possible strategy is to start with: I am encouraged by the number of women in the medical field today who are maintaining successful medical practices in addition to being wives and mothers. I believe that you can only put forth your best in your profession if other areas of your life are equally balanced. One way to do this is by becoming aware of the stresses that will come my way, and discussing it openly with my significant other (or those it may affect). I realize the need of having a strong support system outside of work, and I will use it to keep myself grounded both in my personal and professional life.

Additional Practice Questions:

2.   Are you concerned about the present liability insurance crisis in the U.S.?
3.   Will it affect your decision of a specialty?

4.   *You have the weekend off, but a long-time patient calls and states that she has just been hospitalized and pleads with you to come meet her. She hasn't met the doctor covering your patients this weekend, and states that she wouldn't be comfortable with a new person. However, you had promised your two young children that you would take them to a ski camp that weekend. What would you do?*
5.   *Are you concerned about the declining salary and respect accorded to doctors today?*
6.   *What sacrifices do doctors have to make for their profession?*
7.   *If you suspected that a colleague was abusing pain medications, would you confront him or report him to the State Board? Why?*

Current Events

1. Have the recent political events in the Middle East affected your life?
2. How do you feel about the current economic situation of the country?
3. How do you feel about the President?

Questions for the Admissions Committee

The interview isn't intended to be just a grueling session for the medical school candidate. It is also your opportunity to have any questions answered to determine if this is the right place for you. Once you've read through the brochures provided by the school, compile a list of questions for the interviewers based on any unanswered questions that remain. Consider the following:

1. What percent of your graduating class enters primary care fields as opposed to specialties?
2. Is the format of the curriculum expected to change during the next four years?
3. What research opportunities exist for medical students?
4. Do you offer national or international electives?
5. Do students have access to mentors or advisors? If so, are they clinical faculty or students?
6. What clinical settings are students exposed to - hospitals, ambulatory sites, private clinics?
7. Is there student representation on curriculum committees, policy-making committees, etc?
8. What percentage of your students get into their top choice for residency programs?

Read Medical School Interview Experiences of applicants across the U.S. and Canada: www.studentdoctor.net

Final Thoughts:

Medical school candidates rank the personal interview as the toughest part of the applications process. After all, there aren't many careers that require you to pass a personality test first. However, preparation breeds confidence, and you can successfully navigate through this last obstacle through knowledge, tact and self-assurance. Use the sample answers to the common questions as a model, but rely on your own experiences to provide depth to your answers. Nothing looks more attractive on a candidate than sincerity.

Part 2: Opportunities in Medicine for Distinct Groups

Introduction to Part Two:

Distinct groups are defined here as ethnic minorities and older students. It also includes those who are economically or geographically disadvantaged, interested in a dual career with the Armed Forces, or seeking a degree and specialization beyond an MD. Medical schools are seeking to train diverse groups of individuals to meet the wide-ranging needs of today's society. This part aims to provide the different options for these candidates. It also discusses osteopathic medical school education as an alternative to an MD. Although it is a different route, osteopathic medical schools provide similar education and opportunities for medical practice. This part is for all the candidates who are looking to maximize their chances of admission into medical school by using their special circumstances as an advantage.

Chapter 7: Minorities, Military, Multi-degree and Mature Students

> "People who say it cannot be done should not interrupt those who are doing it."
> - Anonymous

Along the halls of medical schools hang the portraits of all previous graduating classes. A walk past these photos reveals the significant changes that have occurred in the educational system and society over time. Instead of the all-white, predominantly male group shots, today's portraits depict an equal mix of genders, and a variety of ethnicities and ages.

The experience of medical school is rich not only because of its educational content, but because of the inspiring, intelligent and compassionate classmates you will work with during the four years. Medical schools are keenly aware of the need to pick students with different strengths and backgrounds. The following sections focus on such applicants who face unique opportunities and challenges in preparing their applications and going through the admissions process.

What are Options for a Minority or Disadvantaged Student?

Many medical schools offer enrichment programs designed to prepare minority or disadvantaged students for entry into medicine. They may also allow special consideration during the admissions process. Racial minority groups are grossly underrepresented in the medical field across the United States. Underrepresented minorities are defined as African Americans, Native Americans, Mexican Americans and mainland Puerto Ricans. Studies have shown that minority populations feel more comfortable with doctors from their own cultural background, for reasons such as ability to converse in their native language and the physician's capacity to understand the socioeconomic factors that shape the lives and health of their patients. To increase the number of racial populations under-represented in medicine, medical schools have established a Minority Affairs office, and encourage students to apply to their different programs. Their mandate is to aid the efforts of minority students in entering medical school by extending academic help and providing a supportive environment. The wide range of pro-grams offered by each school is too extensive to list in this publication, and stu-dents are advised to contact each medical school directly for more information.

Minority students should not be confused with disadvantaged students. Disadvantaged students fall in the category of economically disadvantaged, or from a rural area of the state that is underrepresented in the physician workforce. At the time that the MCAT is written, ethnic groups currently underrepresented in medicine, and financially disadvantaged students, can indicate their status on the Medical Minority Applicant Registry (Med-MAR). This information is submitted to medical schools and agencies who are interested in increasing the number of minority physicians in practice, and gives them an opportunity to inform the appli-cant about their programs and financial aid resources.

The AAMC publishes a guide for minority student applicants every two years. It includes information on recruitment, admissions, academic support pro-grams, enrichment programs, financial assistance and statistical data on gender and racial/ethnic groups, provided by each medical school. Minority Student Opportunities in United States Medical Schools is available at aamc.org.

There are national programs that provide opportunities for minority students to learn more about medicine, gain research and clinical exposure and receive per-sonalized attention from preparatory programs so that they may become strong medical school or graduate program research candidates.

Preparatory Programs for Minority Students

The Summer Medical Education Program, a national enrichment program through the Robert Wood Johnson Foundation, aims to help motivated students enter medical school by undertaking a 6 week preparatory program during the undergraduate years. Post-baccalaureate students are also encouraged to apply. 63% of students who participated in the program were accepted into medical school.

Eligible students include those committed to diversity, with a background of economic disadvantage, minority racial or ethnic status, or a rural area of resi-dence. Academic qualifications include: overall GPA of 3.00, science GPA of 2.75, combined SAT score of at least 950 or ACT score of at least 20.

Students chosen into the program receive free tuition, housing and meals at one of 11 medical schools across the U.S. *The participating programs include:*

University of Alabama School of Medicine	Fisk University and Vanderbilt University Medical Center
Baylor College of Medicine and Rice University	New Jersey Medical School
Case Western Reserve University School of Medicine	University of Virginia School of Medicine
Chicago Summer Science Enrichment Program	University of Washington School of Medicine and the University of Arizona College of Medicine Consortium
Columbia University College of Physicians and Surgeons	Yale University School of Medicine
Duke University School of Medicine	

For more information on the Summer Medical Enrichment Program, email: smep@aamc.org, or call 1 (866) 304-SMEP (7637).

Exposure to Research Medicine for Minority Students

Undergraduate minority students who have completed 2 or more years of college and have an interest in research medicine can participate in summer programs sponsored by the Leadership Alliance, which is a group of 31 academic and research institutions. Interested candidates are invited to submit applications for an opportunity to work as a summer intern in a research laboratory under a faculty advisor for a period of 9 to 10 weeks. For example, in 2004, John Hopkins University offered 60 internship positions - divided equally among the Basic Science Institute, Division of Pulmonary and Critical Care Medicine, and the Bloomberg School of Public Health. A stipend and living accommodations are provided.

The program's goal is to encourage students to consider academic or research careers in science, medicine and public health by pursuing graduate studies or PhD programs. This program is not suited for individuals interested solely in clinical medicine.

Institutions that participate in this program include:

Brooklyn College
Brown University

Claflin University
Clark Atlanta University

Columbia University
Cornell University

Dartmouth College
Delaware State University

Harvard University
Howard University

Hunter College
Johns Hopkins University

Montana State University-Bozeman
Morehouse College

Morgan State University
New York University

Prairie View A&M University
Princeton University

Southern University at Baton Rouge
Spelman College

Stanford University
Tougaloo College

Tufts University
University of Colorado at Boulder

University of Maryland
University of Miami

University of Pennsylvania
University of Puerto Rico

University of Texas at San Antonio
Xavier University of Louisiana

Yale University

For more information on the Summer Research Early Identification Program at Leadership Alliance, visit: http://www.theleadershipalliance.org.

Financial Aid for Minority Applicants

In addition to the private grants and scholarships awarded by medical schools to entering minority students. National Medical Fellowships is an organization dedicated to providing financial assistance for minority doctors in medicine, It is part of an effort to bring medical care to underserved populations. Need-based scholarships in amounts of $500 to $10,000 have been awarded in the past, and numerous merit awards are also available. Students can contact the organization at: http://www.nmf-online.org.

National Medical Fellowships supports students who are United States citizens of African-American, mainland Puerto Rican, Mexican-American, American Indian, Native Alaskan or Native Hawaiian descent, and are enrolled in schools that grant a Doctor of Medicine, or Doctor of Osteopathic Medicine, degree in the United States and Puerto Rico.

What if I Want to Practice in the Military?

Candidates interested in a medical career within the Department of Defense, either in the Army, Navy, Air Force or Public Health Service, can combine their interests at The Uniformed Services University of the Health Sciences and the F. Edward Hébert School of Medicine. The institution began accepting students in

1976 for medical training. The curriculum focuses on the skills needed for effective medical care in any given military situation, such as military medicine, preventive medicine, tropical medicine, and disaster medicine.

Application for the School of Medicine is similar to applying to any other medical school in the U.S. Both civilian and uniformed services personnel who are committed to military medicine are eligible to apply. Applicants must also meet the requirements for joining or continuing in the Armed Forces. Students who are accepted are provided free tuition for all four years of medical school in return for service after receiving medical licensure.

Other admissions criteria include: age older than 18, American citizenship, sound moral character, and an undergraduate degree from an accredited school in the U.S., Canada or Puerto Rico. Pre-requisite courses include: one year each of General or Inorganic Chemistry, Organic Chemistry, Physics, Biology, English, and one semester of Calculus. Students need to write the MCAT exam to be considered for admission.

For further information, contact:

Uniformed Services University of the Health Sciences
Admissions Office
F. Edward Hébert School of Medicine
4301 Jones Bridge Road, Room A1041
Bethesda MD 20814-4799
Toll free: 1-800-772-1743
Web site: http://www.usuhs.mil

Armed Forces Health Professions Scholarship Program

Students are eligible to apply for the Health Professions Scholarship Program once they have been accepted into a medical school in the United States. The Scholarship program provides full tuition, fees, books, supplies, and health insurance while in medical school. In addition, a stipend of $1100-1200 is provided monthly for 10 and a half months, followed by one and a half months of paid active duty as a second lieutenant during the summers of medical school. In return, medical students agree to a term of service equal to the number of years of scholarship received. Service begins following internship and residency. For further information on the program, contact your nearest Uniformed Services Recruiters, or visit: www.navy.com, www.goarmy.com, www.airforce.com.

What are Options for an Older Student?

It is unfortunate that applicants as young as the mid-thirties to forties are referred to as 'older applicants'. The term has developed out of comparison with the age of a typical medical school applicant. The median age of a first year medical student has been 24 for the past 10 years. However, it is not uncommon to find students in the mid to late thirties, and occasionally forties, in almost all medical schools across the United States and Canada. Shifting careers between the third and fourth decades of life is never an easy decision, particularly in a field such as medicine where the training process is lengthier than all other professions.

It takes dedication and a strong desire to start the process of applying to medical school, as these non-traditional applicants face additional challenges compared to the average medical school applicant. These include, but are not limited to:

- Leaving behind the security of a stable income in order to study
- Taking undergraduate courses again to become eligible to apply to medical school
- Overcoming the negative remarks of friends and relatives who may not understand your motivations
- Delaying any financial rewards for 4 years while in medical school, and then earning a resident's modest salary for the length of the residency
- Devising financial plans to support your family and pay the mortgage while in school
- Finding time during medical training to maintain a family life

Despite the non-traditional approach to becoming a doctor, older candidates can become ideal medical school candidates. They already have the advantage of being an individual with more life experiences than the average applicant. If they've led an interesting life, then they will stand out even more among the thousands of other applicants. Medical schools do not judge such applicants by separate criteria, but they do pay attention to their life and work experiences.

While medical schools legally cannot discriminate based on age, it has been argued that a physician who starts training at a later point in life will practice for a shorter span prior to retirement. In addition, since state governments often subsidize medical education, it is more cost-effective to train a younger physician who can practice for a greater number of years. Similar arguments had been used in the past against female physicians, citing that the responsibilities of child-bearing and motherhood might hinder their ability to be able physicians. But perceptions change, and the reality now is that there are more female than male medical school students enrolled in the entering classes across the United States. If you are dedicated to becoming a physician, do not be dissuaded by arguments that you will be at a disadvantage for medical school. Good physicians come from all walks of life, and maturity brings commitment and a valuable insight into the human condition.

Older students tend to enter primary care specialties such as Family Practice and Internal Medicine.

In addition to possessing all the qualities sought by Admissions Committees, the older applicant needs to demonstrate that the decision to enter medicine has been a well-considered and realistic thought process. Applicants will be asked about provisions that they have made for other responsibilities in their lives, such as family and financial commitments. The techniques for gaining admission, as discussed in Part I, are just as relevant for the older student, and should be reviewed carefully.

A competitive MCAT score and GPA are necessary for admission. An applicant with slightly lower scores should not hesitate to apply if they feel their application is balanced out by achievements in other fields, or unique life experiences. Since each applicant is considered on an individual basis, the candidate has a strong chance of being viewed favorably by some schools. The applicant should ensure that he has met the other required criteria, such as evidence of a commitment to medicine through volunteer work or other experiences within healthcare.

Candidates should be able to answer the following ten questions confidently as they prepare to apply.

- What attracts me to medical school?
- What have I done to explore the healthcare field as a career?
- Why did I make this decision now, and not 10 years earlier?
- Where do I see myself 10 years from now?
- What do my spouse and family members think about this decision?
- Will I be able to find the financial resources for medical school tuition, mortgage payments, childcare, relocation costs, car payments, etc?
- Can I afford not to have any earnings for the next four years?
- Will I be able to meet my responsibilities as a parent while in medical school and residency?
- Do I have the ability to work with and learn from medical students and doctor younger than me?
- What will I do if I don't get accepted into medical school?

Preparing for Medical School for the Older Candidate

Many older candidates have been out of the educational arena for many years prior to applying for medical school, and this often becomes their weak spot. Since the GPA and MCAT score heavily influence the decision of medical school Admissions Committees, you should ensure that your academic abilities and potential are accurately reflected by your marks. Post-baccalaureate programs are a good option for students who wish to demonstrate recent academic achievement, and those who require additional pre-medical courses to fulfill the prerequisite requirements.

Post-baccalaureate programs offer programs, courses and guidance for individuals who hold a Bachelor's degree but need further academic work to become eligible for medical school. All candidates interested in pursuing a post-baccalaureate program should meet with a pre-medical counselor or an admissions advisor at the medical school of their choice to identify the type of program best suited to their needs. In addition, advisors can provide assistance in reviewing a candidate's academic record and highlighting areas that require improvement. Some post-baccalaureate have special arrangements with affiliated medical schools, where a number of their students are given preference for entry.

There are different types of post-baccalaureate programs available. Some are focused on strengthening the applications of minority candidates, others focus on providing courses for students who have fulfilled little, if any, prerequisite Science courses, and still others that offer degree programs. Students should be aware that enrolling in a graduate degree program, such as a Masters or PhD, at many universities requires that the degree be completed prior to applying to medical school. Medical school Admissions Committees do not look favorably upon students who show intention of jumping ship from graduate school into medical school.

Post-baccalaureate programs can be expensive, and students should compare several programs to find one that meets their needs. Apart from such programs, students can also take courses at universities without being part of a formal program in order to fulfill the prerequisite requirements for medical school.

Alternative Routes into Medicine for Older Candidates

Osteopathic medical schools have a larger proportion of older candidates in their student body population in comparison to allopathic medical schools. They focus on teaching a holistic view of health and preventative medicine. The average age of the entering class tend to be higher, and these schools invite applications from older and second-career students. For more information on Osteopathic Medicine, see Chapter 8.

Older students who are unable to gain entrance to an allopathic or osteopathic medical school in the United States also have the option of entering a foreign medical school, in locations such as the Caribbean, Europe, India and South America. For further information on foreign medical education, refer to Part 3.

Combined MD-PhD, MD-JD, MD-MBA, MD-MPH Programs
A group of candidates who deserve special mention are those looking for more than a medical degree. Increasingly, schools are offering the chance of combining medicine with research, law, public health and other newly emerging fields.

MD-PhD programs

Students interested in a career in research and clinical medicine can complete an MD and PhD degree through integrated programs offered at a number of medical schools. 39 U.S. medical schools are funded for the Medical Scientist Training Program (MSTP) by the National Institutes of Health. These programs are usually 7-8 years in length, and focus on preparing doctors with strong research skills in investigating disease mechanisms. MD/PhD graduates have the advantage of pursuing research medicine in an academic or clinical setting upon graduation.

Candidates have to fulfill admissions criteria for medical school as well as the doctoral program to be accepted into a combined program. Fellowships may be available through individual programs to fund tuition and provide a modest stipend for the duration of training. Most programs begin with two years of medical school, followed by graduate courses, lab work and thesis research, and end with the final two years of medical school consisting of hospital clinical clerkships.

Information on admission requirements should be obtained from individual schools. For further information on MSTP, contact:

National Institutes of Health MSTP Administrator
Room 905
Westwood Building
Bethesda, MD 20892
(301) 594-7744

Combined MD-JD programs

There are presently 15 combined MD-JD programs offered in the U.S. Students can complete a combined Doctor of Medicine degree and Juris Doctor of Law degree in six to seven years. Students need to fulfill admissions requirements for both medical and law school in order to be considered for the combined program. These include writing the Medical College Admission Test as well as the Law School Admission Test.

Such a program may appeal to students wishing to pursue a legal career with an in-depth knowledge of medical issues, academic medicine, forensic medicine, health care administration, and public and governmental policy development.

Combined MD-MBA Programs

Combining medicine and business is becoming a popular option for medical students. 40 universities across the U.S. provide the option of completing a combined Doctor of Medicine degree and a Masters in Business Administration in five years. Some schools may allow medical students to enroll in the MBA program during the second year of medical studies, as long as a passing grade is maintained in all medical courses. Other schools may require joint forms to be filled out at the time of initial application, and students may be required to write the Medical College Admission Test as well as the Graduate Management Admission Test.

The combined program option may appeal to candidates interested in learning about management of healthcare. The knowledge gained in business school can help doctors run their clinical practices. They can also use their business skills to provide consulting services to corporations on issues of healthcare products and services.

Combined MD-MPH Programs

Students interested in gaining a wider perspective on public health, environmental health and social and behavioral issues in healthcare within their medical training can elect for a combined Doctor of Medicine and Masters in Public Health program. The program can be completed in as little as four years at some schools, which is usually the length of time required for medical school alone, or in five years if students choose to pursue additional projects within the MPH program. Career opportunities for doctors with a background in public health include management positions within healthcare organizations, such as hospitals, health departments or private health corporations. Graduates can also choose to do research for state health agencies and federal bodies such as the National Institutes of Health and Centre for Disease Control. Fellowships in Preventive Medicine and Occupational Medicine later in residency allow graduates to carve a niche as experts within the public health field.

Other unique fields for combined degree programs are emerging rapidly, and the following are just a few examples:

Yale University
MD-MAR: Doctor of Medicine and Master of Arts in Religion
MD-Div: Doctor of Medicine and Master of Divinity
Virginia Commonwealth University School of Medicine
MD-MHA: Doctor of Medicine and Masters in Health Administration
Vanderbilt University
MD/MEd: Doctor of Medicine and Master of Education degree
MD/MTS: Doctor of Medicine and Master of Theological Studies
MD/MSCS: Doctor of Medicine and Master of Science in Computer Science
MD/MDiv: Doctor of Medicine and Master of Divinity degree
MD/MSBMI: Doctor of Medicine and Master of Science in Biomedical Informatics degree
MD/MSBME: Doctor of Medicine and Master of Science in Biomedical Engineering degree

Final Thoughts:

Diversity is being embraced by medical schools throughout North America, and this is good news for everyone who isn't the typical 24 year old pre-medical university student. Older candidates, minorities, Armed Forces personnel, or those seeking more than just your basic MD, such as a dual degree in law, business or public health, have more opportunities than ever before to fulfill their aspirations of becoming a doctor. As much as you may want to enter medicine, medical schools are also looking for the right mix in student population. Your strengths and interests may not parallel those of the next candidate, but they don't need to either. Make your differences your calling card, and allow them to distinguish you.

Chapter 8: Alternative to an MD: Doctor of Osteopathic Medicine

> "What's in a name? That which we call a rose by any
> other name would smell as sweet."
> - Shakespeare

During my Intensive Care Unit rotation as an intern, I had the chance to work with two Critical Care Attending Physicians. One was an MD and the other was a DO. They worked side by side on the same patient problems, and performed the same procedures. Although they had started their education on different paths, they now practiced identical careers.

Few students may be familiar with the field of osteopathy. It was founded in 1874 by Dr. Andrew Taylor Still, who felt the need to incorporate a holistic view of the patient's problems into the traditional medical model.

The basic philosophies of osteopathic medicine are the following:

- medicine should be practiced with attention to the whole person rather than individual diseased organs
- an imbalance of the musculoskeletal system influences symptoms and diseases, which can be alleviated with osteopathic manipulative techniques
- the body has an ability to heal itself, and the objectives of osteopathic medicine are to remove any impediments to the body's healing mechanisms

- preventive medicine is a key element in healthcare

Training as a Doctor of Osteopathic Medicine (DO) provides the same opportunities for medical practice in the United States as graduating from an allopathic medical school. The admission process is similar, and the main curriculum difference is that DO's receive over 200 hours training in osteopathic manipulative medicine. Students are required to take the MCAT prior to application. All applications to osteopathic medical schools take place through a centralized process known as the American Association of Colleges of Osteopathic Medicine Application Service (AACOMAS). Further information can be found at https://aacomas.aacom.org.

Since the philosophies of osteopathic and allopathic medicine are slightly different, spend time with professionals in both fields before determining which type of medical school is a better match for you. If you don't feel limited by either school of thought, consider applying to both programs to increase your odds of acceptance.

Following four years of education at an accredited osteopathic medical school, students have the option of pursuing a residency in osteopathic medicine, or applying for an allopathic residency in any specialty.

DO's comprise five percent of practicing physicians in the U.S. today, and the twenty schools of osteopathic medicine accept approximately 2500 students annually. Up to one quarter of enrolled students are considered non-traditional candidates. Many have worked previously in other fields, such as law and business, and have different experiences and strengths. Osteopathic schools of medicine look for similar criteria to other medical schools, namely, strong interpersonal skills, diverse strengths, solid academic achievements and extracurricular work in the healthcare field. In addition, many colleges expect that the candidate is familiar with the principles and practice of osteopathic medicine, and are able to provide a letter of reference from a practicing D.O.

For the majority of osteopathic schools, pre-requisite courses include: Biology, Inorganic Chemistry, Organic Chemistry, Physics, English, with additional requirements of Behavioral Sciences and Calculus at select schools.

Some osteopathic schools offer the opportunity of a combined degree program, with completion of a Bachelor of Science and Doctor of Osteopathic Medicine degree in 7 years. See Chapter 2 for more information.

Osteopathic Medical School Curriculum

An osteopathic medical school curriculum covers the courses taught in allopathic medical schools, with additional instruction on the practice of osteopathic principles throughout the four years. First year courses include Anatomy, Physiology, Microbiology, Histology, Pathology, Clinical Skills, Biochemistry and Pathology. The second year focuses on organ specific systems, such as Cardiology, as well as Ethics, Family Practice, Pediatrics and Gerontology. The last two years are spent in clinical clerkships at hospitals, doing rotations in Internal Medicine, Surgery, Obstetrics, Gynecology, Anesthesiology, Pediatrics, Family Practice, Orthopedics, Psychiatry and Radiology, among other specialties. Students also work with patients in community health centers and doctor's offices.

Licensing Requirements

To be licensed as an Osteopathic Physician, candidates need to pass three exams set by the National Board of Osteopathic Medical Examiners. The Comprehensive Osteopathic Licensure Examination (COMLEX) consists of three levels. Level I is written at the end of the second year of medical school, Level II in the fourth year, and Level III at the end of the internship year. Osteopathic medical students also need to write the USMLE Steps I and II in order to pursue an allopathic residency, and Step III at the end of internship. At the end of residency, D.O.'s take exams set by the Specialty Board of their intended field of practice.

Cost of an Osteopathic Medical Education

The tuition varies significantly for in-state versus out-of-state residents. For in-state residents, tuition varies from a low of approximately $7000 to more than $30,000. For out-of-state residents, tuition varies from $19,000 to $45,000. Various loans, grants and scholarships are available from the federal government, National Health Service Corps, Armed forces, minority agencies, and private college funds to help finance tuition.

The Pros and Cons of a D.O. degree

A DO degree provides the same opportunities as an allopathic medical degree for licensure as a practicing physician across the United States. Primary care specialties continue to be in demand, and DO's are ideally suited to contribute in this arena due to the strong training they receive in preventive medicine and holistic care. In one distinct way, graduates of osteopathic medicine have more options available to them on graduation, as they can choose to continue with an allopathic residency, or an osteopathic residency. The colleges offering osteopathic training are well-established, and receive national scholarships and funding just as traditional medical schools do. Upon licensure, an Osteopathic Doctor receives the same compensation as an MD for similar work.

However, unlike an MD degree obtained in the U.S., a DO degree may not be recognized in all countries. Candidates should check with the Ministry of Health of individual countries if they are interested in practicing outside the U.S. Students have limited choice among colleges, as there are only twenty schools nationwide, in contrast to the 125 allopathic medical schools. Students who pursue allopathic residencies need to write additional exams (USMLE Steps 1, 2 and 3) in addition to the licensing exams for osteopathic medicine. Some allopathic residency programs may not consider DO's to be competitive for all residency and specialty positions. Additionally, many patients are not familiar of the distinction between an MD and DO, and DOs may find that they have to repeatedly explain their credentials.

Final Thoughts:

An MD degree is not the only passport to a medical practice. Students can increase their options and chances of acceptance by considering schools of osteopathic medicine. Allopathic and osteopathic medical doctors are the only type of 'complete' doctors in the U.S. The similar training allows them to practice in all specialties of medicine. Students should investigate both types of education to assess which is a better match to their philosophies and qualifications.

Part 3: International Medical Schools

Introduction to Part Three:

The competition for medical school admission over the past decade has resulted in many students looking outside the U.S.A. for the opportunity of a medical education. But where are the best schools? How much does it cost? What are the requirements? What are the chances of admission? What are the licensure requirements with a foreign medical degree? Since there isn't a licensing body that oversees foreign medical schools, students need to act as their own advocate when choosing to study abroad. This part covers the basics they need to know before pursuing such a path.

Canadian medical schools are discussed in Chapter 10. Canadian and U.S. medical schools have joint accreditation by the Liaison Committee on Medical Education, and are of equal standard. Those interested in studying in Canada will find information on medical schools and post-graduate training positions.

Chapter 9: Foreign Medical Education: Is it a Viable Alternative?

> Education begins with life
> - Benjamin Franklin

Obtaining a Medical degree outside North America

The desire to become a doctor can be so strong for some individuals that they are willing to move to another country to pursue their dream. This may even mean learning the curriculum in another language. Seeking a foreign medical education is not a new concept. Prior to the establishment of medical academic centers in the United States, students routinely traveled to Europe for a medical education, and brought back their skills. The difference now, though, is that the U.S. offers the best medical training and research facilities that the world has to offer, and the reasons for choosing to study abroad have changed. Common reasons cited by students for seeking a foreign education include:

- Opportunity to experience a new culture
- Finishing a medical degree in as little as 5 years as opposed to 7-8 years in the United States
- Obtaining a medical seat with a lower GPA than that required by U.S. schools
- MCAT isn't required
- Rigorous criteria such as outstanding letters of recommendation and extracurricular experience play a lesser role in gaining admission

- Students can start medical studies without completing any undergraduate work
- Inability to obtain a U.S. medical school seat

For a list of popular foreign medical schools, refer to Appendix B

It is eye-opening to consider that a quarter of practicing physicians in the United States today are international medical graduates. The majority of these physicians were trained in their native countries, and migrated to the U.S. after completing medical school. In many cases, they had also completed post-graduate training and were practicing independently in their native countries. While many countries other than the U.S. and Canada provide superb medical training, these are not the programs that U.S. citizens attend when they elect for a foreign medical education. With few exceptions such as Australia and Ireland, many developed countries have closed their doors or become very selective in providing medical education for citizens of other nations. The result is that a number of for-profit institutions have sprung up, many in poor and developing countries, which aim to attract American and Canadian students to their doors.

The number of U.S. foreign graduates who return to pursue postgraduate training is growing annually, but these candidates may face difficulty obtaining a residency position. It is usually the case that they spend over a year writing the three USMLE Board Exams, and then only half manage to secure a residency spot. Their acceptance rate is similar to those of non-U.S. foreign medical graduates. Only students registered in foreign schools listed in the World Directory of Medical Schools, published by the World Health Organization, are able to transfer to another medical school in the U.S., and are eligible to practice in the U.S. after passing the required exams. The World Directory of Medical Schools is available at http://www.who.int. Students should be aware that inclusion of a medical school in the Directory does not imply any form of accreditation or guarantee of a quality education.

There is a very wide range in the quality of foreign medical education available. Some schools have been set up hastily with the goal of recruiting North American students, and charge exorbitant tuitions. Their admission requirements tend to be lower than other foreign medical schools, such as in England and Australia, which are well-established but selective in their choice of foreign students. Unfortunately, an official, reliable ranking of foreign medical schools has never been attempted, and students have to proceed with caution when considering their choices. Some of the disadvantages of a foreign medical education may include:

- High tuitions (comparable to or higher than a private U.S. medical education)
- Up to half of all graduates do not end up practicing in the U.S. as they fail to pass the licensing exams or to obtain a residency position
- Lack of medical school accreditation by the same standards applied to U.S. schools
- Lack of adequate clinical teaching facilities and staff
- Lack of diagnostic equipment of the same standards as in the U.S.
- Learning medicine in a foreign language
- Unsanitary or uncomfortable living conditions
- Diseases common in the country of study may be different from the U.S.
- Students may not qualify for Federal Student Loans
- Lack of a social support network of family and friends during the stress of medical training
- May not be considered competitive for highly sought residency positions such as Plastic Surgery, Dermatology, and Radiology
- Residency directors often use U.S. clinical experience as major criteria for granting post-graduate training positions
- International medical graduates consistently score lower on the licensing exams compared to American and Canadian graduates

While the disadvantages of a foreign medical education are not meant to dissuade you if you are strongly considering this option, be on the lookout for warning signs as you research these institutions.

Steps to ensuring a quality foreign medical education:

1. Obtain information on the track record of the school

Reputable schools will not hesitate to provide information about their credentials and student performance profiles. Be skeptical of schools that appear to be inflating student scores on Steps 1 and 2, as the reality is that foreign medical graduates have the greatest difficulty in passing these licensing exams compared to American, Canadian and non-U.S. foreign graduates. Ask the school if they have ever been cited by a licensing authority for curriculum deficiencies or placed under sanctions, particularly by the U.S. Also inquire about the percentage of graduates who successfully obtained residency positions. Be skeptical if the school is unable to provide such information, as all schools keep such records. Ensure that the school is recognized in the World Directory of Medical Schools.

Inquire into the school's accreditation. Lastly, inquire if the school has been credentialed by the U.S. Department of Education.

2.   *Find out the language requirements of the curriculum*
Most schools in Europe, with the exception of the United Kingdom and Ireland, offer instruction only in the native language of the country. Some medical colleges provide additional language classes, but this may extend the length of the program by up to 18 months. Others offer an English version of their curriculum in addition to their standard courses, but students can be at a disadvantage with this approach also. It does not address how they would communicate with patients in the clinical years. Working through translators is a frustrating process, and slows down the fast pace expected in the hospital environment.

3.   *Identify if the school offers any clinical training in the U.S.*
For the prospective applicant, it is important to find out if transition back to the U.S. will proceed smoothly at the end of medical school. Medical colleges that offer the latter part of their curriculum in U.S. hospitals offer an advantage, as Residency Directors will feel more confident in the student's abilities to function well in an American hospital. Ask the school for a list of its clinical training sites in the U.S. Some schools leave it up to the student to arrange clerkships in the U.S. rather than having well-established programs with hospitals. It can be difficult to arrange for rotations on an individual basis, especially within teaching hospitals that have residents and students from other medical schools. Community hospitals may be more receptive, but the level of teaching won't be as organized and rigorous as in a teaching hospital.

4.   *Be skeptical of programs that offer credit for previous healthcare experience or offer distance learning*
Some schools entice older and non-traditional students by offering credit for previous experience in the healthcare field. For example, former chiropractors and dentists are assured that their previous knowledge makes them eligible to finish the medical degree in a shorter period, therefore saving tuition and time. While the schools appear to be making special concessions, keep in mind that American and Canadian schools do not give any similar credit. In order to practice in the U.S., students are required by State Boards to attend medical school for a specified period of time. Students who were unsuspecting participants in such schemes have been refused licensure by multiple State Boards. Schools that offer distance learning courses are notorious for being refused State Board licensure also. These programs require student presence on the foreign campus for a very small period of

time, usually only months. Students then return to the U.S. and complete their medical education through distance learning. Unfortunately, while the idea is tempting, medicine simply cannot be learnt in this manner.

Keep in mind that getting into a residency program is not sufficient to obtain licensure as a physician at the end of residency. State Boards will scrutinize your medical school education prior to granting a license, even after you've completed residency.

5.   *Find out if the school is eligible for U.S. Federal Student Loan Programs*

While having the approval of the Federal Government for state loans isn't an assurance of the quality of the program, it is an additional tool that students can use to narrow down the list. It provides reassurance that another governing body has looked into the credentials of the institution. The better schools have qualified for such funding, while none of the less reputable ones are presently eligible. However, there have been cases in the past when Federal Loan Programs were withdrawn from medical colleges, such as in the West Indies and Mexico.

6.   *Ensure that the school provides basic resources- such as a library stocked with the latest editions of medical journals and textbooks, access to medical learning software, and sufficient cadaver quantity.*

While the majority of medical students usually would not think of asking about cadaver quantity and quality when researching schools, it is an important question. In the U.S., the dissection of cadavers forms the basis of learning gross anatomy. Four to six students are usually assigned to a previously unused cadaver. In some foreign locations, there is only one cadaver available for the entire class, or the cadavers have been used multiple times. Cadaveric tissue becomes dry and friable very quickly, and multiple uses guarantee poor quality. In some labs, there aren't any cadavers available at all. Students are asked to suffice with plastic models.

The lack of adequate facilities is a common complaint among foreign medical students. Few schools offer adequate library resources, such as a full range of journals and medical texts. Computer labs appear to fare better, but some schools have had difficulty providing access to students in this area also. Medicine is a field where knowledge changes rapidly, so easy access to journals is a must. Students should not settle for anything less.

7.   *Speak to previous graduates*

Former graduates can be a valuable resource in pointing out advantages and disadvantages of the program. Specifically, ask about living conditions, quality of the instructors, satisfaction with the curriculum, patient population, and access to clerkships in the U.S. If information on the student population is not easily available from the Admissions office, find out if there are a large number of transfer students into the program, which often implies students who failed at their previous medical college. Most importantly, inquire about any difficulties they have experienced with returning to the U.S., writing Board exams, obtaining a residency position, and receiving licensure.

8.   Visit the campus

This step cannot be emphasized strongly enough. Unfortunately, many students fear that they cannot afford the additional expense of a visit prior to enrolling. This, however, is a very small price to pay if it helps to avoid future problems with your medical degree! Students who have chosen schools based on information provided by recruiters and the Admissions office are often sorely disappointed with the reality. The medical campus may be nothing more than a rented, dilapidated building. The free living accommodations provided by the school may be in such bad condition that students prefer to rent elsewhere. These are actual situations that have occurred, and these medical colleges are still in operation.

Visiting the campus will also provide an opportunity to speak with current students and instructors, and attend some classes. Find out the credentials of the instructors. Schools with a large number of full-time faculty tend to be more stable than those that recruit instructors from the U.S. and Canada for a few weeks at a time.

9.   Inquire about the tuition refund policy and financial stability of the school

A substantial amount of money is required by foreign schools before students have had a chance to gain familiarity with the program and find out whether they are satisfied with the quality of the education. Inquire about circumstances under which tuition will be refunded. Some schools will only recompense students if they are unable to continue their education due to an illness.

Medical schools in Mexico, South America and the Caribbean have closed down without much warning in the past when they failed to profit as businesses. Look for stability as one of the most important qualities when researching foreign medical schools.

10. What is the attrition (drop-out) rate of students?

The national average for U.S. medical schools is approximately 3-4%. In foreign medical schools, the rate is often higher than 25%.

For further information on foreign medical schools, visit the website of the American Association of International Medical Graduates at www.aaimg.com. The website provides detailed descriptions of site visits to foreign medical schools.

See Appendix B for a listing of select foreign medical schools that accept American and Canadian students. Unless specified, all the schools have English as the medium of instruction. Where available, length of training, the year that medical instruction started, and the quota for international students have been included.

Cost of a Foreign Medical Education

In the Caribbean schools, tuitions and fees range approximately $100,000 to $150,000 for a four year education. Students will also have additional costs of housing, food, health insurance, liability insurance, textbooks, travel, local transportation, supplies, exam costs and personal expenses. These costs can amount up to an additional $50,000.

Eastern European nations tend to be less expensive, but vary from school to school. The course of instruction is in the official languages of the country. Individual schools should be contacted for further information. Contact information can be found in the World Directory of Medical Schools (http://www.who.int).

Licensing Requirements

Foreign medical graduates are required to pass a number of tests and submit credentials for verification before certification is obtained from the Educational Commission for Foreign Medical Graduates (ECFMG). Medical graduates need to submit their last medical school transcript and medical degree. These are then submitted by ECFMG to the institution that granted the documents to check authenticity. Only schools listed in the International Medical Education Directory (http://imed.ecfmg.org) are recognized by ECFMG. This step is necessary if graduates intend on applying for residency in the U.S.

The required exams include an assessment of the candidate's English speaking skills, as well as the United States Medical Licensing Exam Step 1 and 2. The Test of English as a Foreign Language (TOEFL) costs $130 and can be taken at any Educational Testing Centre throughout the U.S. As of 2004, students who plan on writing the USMLE Step 2 are not required to write the TOEFL, as the Clinical Skills portion of the exam suffices as a test for English language skills also.

The Clinical Skills Assessment (CSA) exam, previously required only of foreign medical graduates, is now mandatory for U.S. medical students as well. Instead of being a separate ECFMG requirement, it has been incorporated in the USMLE Step 2 since 2004. The CSA tests a candidate's ability to obtain a history, perform a clinical exam, and arrive at a diagnosis. Examinees are also required to answer patient questions, provide counseling and formulate plans for workup of the patient's condition. The part of patients is played by actors, who are referred to as 'standardized patients'. The student encounters one patient per station, and there are ten to twelve stations over an eight hour period. Case scenarios are similar to those found in clinical rotations during medical school, and are taken from the fields of Internal Medicine, Surgery, Pediatrics, Psychiatry, Family Medicine, Obstetrics and Gynecology. As part of the USMLE Step 2, the test costs $1200. The USMLE Steps 1 and 2 scores can make the difference between gaining admission to a reputable residency program or an average one. Many foreign medical graduates take commercial preparation courses in an effort to ensure competitive marks.

TIP:
U.S. foreign medical graduates can choose to write the USMLE Step 3 prior to applying for residency. Although it isn't required until after internship, a good score is looked upon favorably by Medical Directors, and helps in obtaining a residency position.

Before You Leave the Country, Do This!

It may be tempting for students to pack their bags and look towards foreign shores if they've been turned down once already in the U.S. However, it is not recommended that they consider foreign medical schools unless they have been unsuccessful two or even three times. Even then, it is important to consider the reasons for rejection. Each candidate needs to honestly find out the reasons for not being selected. Are there striking deficiencies in the application? Have Admissions Committees determined that the student lacks the motivation or ability to pursue medical training? Did the candidate simply apply to the wrong schools? The reasons for rejection are numerous, and usually not very clear. It is important to consider each aspect of the application carefully, and improve on it prior to giving up on an American medical education.

In order to pinpoint the weaknesses in your application, review the criteria outlined for a successful application in Part 1, and note down areas that you feel have worked against you. Then, speak with your premedical counselor, admissions advisors at medical schools or the Dean of Admissions to get an objective view. Once you have highlighted some areas where your credentials require improvement, develop an approach to transforming them into areas of strength for the next application year.

Academic performance:

How does your overall and science GPA compare with that of accepted candidates? The average science GPA of a successful candidate tends to be over 3.5/4.0. Keep in mind that this is an average only. Many candidates gain admission with a lower GPA as well. If schools had considered your grades competitive, you would have been invited to interviews in previous years. If you weren't, it appears that your application is not passing the initial screen of competitive grades and MCAT scores. Students in this category should consider post-baccalaureate programs as ways of bolstering their academic performance. While the additional time commitment is expensive, it can be done on a part-time basis while working. Students should choose post-baccalaureate programs that have affiliations with medical schools, and have a high rate of acceptance. Post-baccalaureate programs will require dedication and single-minded determination, and only the best candidates will be successful in their goals. The best part of some programs is that medical schools will consider these individuals before considering the general pool of applicants.

Graduate school is also a popular option for students who don't succeed on their first attempt into medical school. While graduate studies won't prepare you for the clinical work of medicine, it is an advantage when considering a research tract in addition to clinical duties. Be aware that many medical schools will not consider you until you have finished your Masters degree, which may take up to two years or longer. In addition, some schools do not consider the grades obtained in graduate school when calculating the overall and science GPA. It remains a good option for candidates with a genuine interest in their chosen field of study, as long as it isn't being done only for the purpose of gaining entry into medicine.

MCAT performance:

As a general rule, scores above 10 on each section of the MCAT is considered competitive. If your MCAT performance falls short of the mark, the first step is to determine if it reflects your actual abilities, or if given extra time and preparation, it is possible to improve on your first attempt. If the latter is true, then consider dedicating four months to studying, and if finances allow, joining an MCAT preparation course.

Extracurricular Activities:

Medical schools like to see that you have extended yourself beyond academics in preparation for medical school. In particular, they will note if you used your spare time in the past to learn more about healthcare. If your application demonstrates a lack of prior interest in medicine, Admissions Committees will question your level of dedication. Start working to correct this right now. Choose a volunteer job that excites you, such as working with children or in the Emergency Department. Approach physicians or Science instructors involved in research, and offer your time and skills as a co-researcher to a project. The opportunities are endless, but they require a pro-active attitude.

A friend with a 96% grade average decided during the third year of his Biochemistry studies that the logical career choice would be medicine. He had all the prerequisite courses, reference letters that spoke highly of his intellect and research abilities, MCAT scores in the 12-13 range but no extracurricular involvement. He obtained many interviews, but was rejected from all the top programs in the country. One medical school did accept him, and he now practices as a General Internist. So why do I mention him? He confesses to feeling dissatisfied with the nature of the work, and feels that prior exposure to medicine may have led him to reconsider his career decision.

Reference letters:

Review Chapter 5 on obtaining the best letters of recommendation. If you plan on approaching the same individuals again for recommendation, speak with them openly about how you plan on strengthening your application this year. Ask for their input also, and follow up on any suggestions they might have.

Interview:

Many unsuccessful candidates feel that their applications were very competitive, and it was the interview that was the decisive factor. Students who do not interview well should try to isolate their weak points with help from objective friends, mentors and the premedical advisor. The only way to become comfortable with interviews is to do as many mock sessions as possible. Videotape the sessions, and critique them to pinpoint areas of improvement. There are only a handful of topics that are usually brought up in a medical school interview, and students should familiarize themselves with the common themes. Review Chapter 6 for interview tips.

Choice of schools:

It can be tempting to apply only to schools with outstanding reputations, but thousands of other candidates will be doing the same thing. Names that should be on your list include all schools within your home state, as they offer the best chances of admission by having reserved seats for state residents. Study the Medical School Admission Requirements publication to determine the average grades and MCAT scores for accepted applicants, and apply to the schools that fall within your range. Study the MSAR to find schools where the bulk of students from your state get accepted. Students often apply to 'safe' schools as well, where the student's academic qualifications, such as MCAT scores and grades, exceed the average for accepted students at these schools. Do include a few of these schools. Additionally, if you have a special interest, such as rural health or research, or belong to a minority group, apply to all the programs that are looking for students with your unique background.

Final Thoughts:

Foreign medical schools can be an option for some individuals. Students should try to identify schools that offer a curriculum comparable to Canada and the U.S. This isn't an easy task, but by using the pointers above, you can improve the odds of obtaining a quality education. Refer to Appendix B for a listing of select popular foreign schools that accept North American students. A medical school education is an investment in you. Choose wisely.

Chapter 10: Getting a Canadian Medical Education

I never let my schooling interfere with my education.
- Mark Twain

Canadian medical schools offer a four year medical degree program leading to an MD. There are seventeen medicals schools in Canada. Each year, approximately 1400 medical student seats are available, with preference given to Canadian citizens and provincial residents.

The criteria for gaining admission into a Canadian medical school are as discussed in Part 1. Academic achievement, MCAT scores, extracurricular activities, research experience and healthcare exposure are all used as to evaluate candidates. Medical schools in Canada and the U.S. follow similar teaching methods and curriculums. It is not surprising, then, that Canadian and American medical education are considered equivalent. The Liaison Committee on Medical Education accredits schools in both countries.

There isn't a centralized system in place for submitting applications to all medical schools in Canada, so most schools need to be contacted directly for an admissions package. Six medical schools within Ontario are the exception to this rule. The Ontario Medical School Application Service (OMSAS) provides a centralized method of applying to McMaster University, University of Ottawa, Queen's University, University of Toronto, University of Western Ontario, and the newly established Northern Ontario Medical School. Instead of submitting separate applications and academic records to each school, students need to submit them only once to OMSAS. Medical schools have separate and distinct requirements for admission, so students need to ensure that they meet these qualifications first. For further information on OMSAS, visit http://www.ouac.on.ca/omsas or write to:

OMSAS
Ontario Universities' Application Centre
170 Research Lane
Guelph ON N1G 5E2

IMPORTANT DATES FOR OMSAS
July: Online application becomes available
Mid-September: Online registration ends
October: Deadline for applications and document submission
End of May: First date for provisional offers of admission
June: Deadline for final transcripts to be received
July: Firm acceptances are sent out

Undergraduate course requirements

The pre-requisite course requirements for Canadian medical schools are as discussed in Part 1. Some schools do not specify any pre-requisites, and look at the overall GPA when assessing academic achievement. In general, pre-requisites and recommended courses, include: 1 year of General Biology, Biochemistry, General Chemistry, Organic Chemistry, English, and Physics. Some schools also recommend Physiology, Psychology, Sociology or Anthropology, and Statistics or Calculus.

Competitive scores on the MCAT are 10 and above for Verbal Reasoning, Physical and Biological Sciences. Minimum grade point average requirements in schools that give preference to provincial residents is 3.3/4.0, and higher for out-of-province residents.

International Students

International medical students are eligible to apply to eleven out of the seventeen schools. However, out of these eleven, three have strict criteria for the international medical students they will consider. The University of Calgary will only accept students from countries with which it has a contractual partnership, such as Brunei and Malaysia. U.S. students do not qualify. The University of Ottawa and Queen's University only consider non-Canadians if they are the children of medical school alumni. An additional three require comprehension of French. Therefore, out of the eleven that do consider foreign students, a non-French speaking American medical school applicant can realistically hope for admission in only five out of the seventeen schools.

While the tuition at a Canadian school can be considerably less compared to a private medical education in the U.S., American students should not look towards Canada as a second choice if they fail to gain acceptance at an American medical college. The reasons are that there are very few positions available for international students, and the academic requirements are just as demanding. The GPA and MCAT scores of accepted students are often higher than that required at an average American medical school. Many Canadian students who cannot obtain a spot in Canada head to the U.S., Caribbean islands or Europe for a medical education.

Students interested in applying to McMaster University and the University of Toronto should contact each school directly for application information. While McMaster University has its own International Applicant Pool, it was temporarily on hold in 2004, and students were advised to apply through OMSAS. International students are judged by different criteria compared to local residents. Admissions criteria, particularly the minimum GPA, change over time, so students should contact each school for the latest eligibility information prior to submitting an application.

International students accepted into a Canadian medical school will have to fulfill the Government of Canada requirements for studying in the country. They will need a student visa, and may need to obtain an entry visa too, depending on their citizenship. They will have to show proof of acceptance into full-time studies, and demonstrate adequate financial resources to sustain tuition and living expenses. There may also be provincial requirements. Quebec, for example, requires students to obtain a Certificat d'acceptation du Gouvernement du Québec (a Quebec government certificate of acceptance).

For more information on Canadian medical schools, refer to Appendix C.

Getting into a Canadian Residency

How the Residency Match Works in Canada
The Canadian Resident Matching Service, CaRMS, is the Canadian equivalent of

the Electronic Residency Application Service (ERAS) and the National Residency Matching Program (NRMP) in the U.S. It is a centralized service that allows graduating medical students to apply for a residency position, and match with postgraduate residency positions. Couples can also enter the Match together, stating their choices for residency programs and locations. The Match attempts to find suitable programs for both candidates within their preferred specialties and geographic locations.

Candidates submit all their application materials to CaRMS, which distributes them to individual residency programs indicated by the student. Students can choose as many different specialties and programs as they wish to be considered for. Following interviews, applicants and Program Directors create a rank order list. CaRMS follows a mathematical algorithm to create a match between students and programs. Candidates who fail to match to a program are advised of their unmatched status two days before Match Day, and can start preparing for the Second Iteration Match. Université Laval, Université de Sherbrooke, and Université de Montréal do not participate in CaRMS.

There are some distinct differences between the U.S. and Canadian Match Programs. While all eligible applicants participate in the National Match in the U.S., the Canadian Match occurs in two iterations. The First Iteration Match is open only to final year Canadian medical students. In some provinces, U.S. medical students who are Canadian citizens or permanent residents may also be considered. They compete for all the open residency spots. Any remaining spots are transferred to the Second Iteration Match. At this point, all other eligible applicants are invited to apply. These independent applicants include unmatched candidates from the First Iteration, previous Canadian medical school graduates with some post-graduate training, U.S. students, and foreign medical school graduates. Since only a limited number of spots are available, the competition in the Second Iteration is intense. There are approximately 3.5 applicants for every position available. International medical graduates can apply outside of CaRMS to individual International Medical Graduate programs in British Columbia, Alberta, Ontario and Quebec. U.S. graduates may have better odds applying through programs that reserve a quota for Americans, such as McGill University. Visit carms.ca for further information.

Steps Involved in Obtaining a Canadian Residency Position:

On-line registration for Match at www.carms.ca in August/September

Registered candidates receive a token (a personal identification number) which permits online application for the Match

Candidates submit the following documents to CaRMS: autobiographical statement, curriculum vitae, photographs, publication abstracts (if applicable), undergraduate and medical school transcripts, Dean's letter and reference letters

Students indicate the residency programs that they wish to be considered for, and await interview calls

Personal interviews take place either in the candidate's city, or the site of the residency program

Students and residency programs submit their final ranking to CaRMS

Match Day occurs in February/March. Students find out which program they will attend for post-graduate studies

Unmatched students, U.S. candidates and International Medical Graduates enter the Second Iteration

Second Iteration Match Day occurs in April

Resident Salaries and Benefits:

The salary range for Post Graduate Year 1 (PGY-1) residents varies among provinces, with the highest salaries offered in Ontario, Manitoba, Alberta and British Columbia. Each additional year of experience entitles them to a higher salary. They are also provided with 4 weeks annual vacation, educational leave, meal allowance, maternity leave, partial or complete life insurance, disability insurance, and dental and health insurance benefits.

Residency Level	Range of Salary
PGY-1	$35,000-$44,000
PGY-2	$38,000-$49,000
PGY-3	$41,000-$53,000
PGY-4	$44,000-$57,000
PGY-5	$48,000-$62,000
PGY-6	$51,000-$66,000
PGY-7	$58,000-$70,000

Data Source: Canadian Residency Matching Service

Length of Residency Programs:

Each specialty in Canada is licensed by the Royal College of Physicians and Surgeons of Canada. The length of residency programs varies, and differs from training requirements in the United States. There are no separate preliminary and categorical programs. Students matched to a program complete their entire residency training within the program's facilities.

Length of Specialty Training:

Following medical school, the years of post-graduate training for specialties are as follow:

Two years
Family Practice

Four years
Hematological Pathology (Lab Medicine)
Pediatrics
General Internal Medicine

Five years
Anatomical Pathology
Nuclear Medicine
Anesthesiology
Obstetrics/Gynecology
Community Medicine

Occupational Medicine
Integrated Community Medicine and Rural Family Practice
Ophthalmology
Dermatology
Orthopedic surgery
Diagnostic Radiology
Otolaryngology
Emergency Medicine
Physical Medicine and Rehabilitation
General Pathology (Lab Medicine)
Plastic Surgery
General Surgery
Psychiatry
Medical Genetics
Radiation Oncology
Neurology Urology
Pediatric Neurology

Six years
Cardiac SurgeryNeurosurgery

Canadians seeking U.S. Residency Positions

A small number of Canadian medical school graduates seek graduate training in a residency program in the U.S. each year. Reasons for such a move include the greater number of residency spots available for each specialty, relocating to be closer to family or spouse, desire to train at a specific, prominent hospital or inability to obtain the residency of choice in Canada. Canadians are not considered as Foreign Medical Graduates, and do not need their credentials verified by the Education Commission for Foreign Medical Graduates when seeking a residency position in the U.S. They will need to write the USMLE Steps 1 and 2 to be considered.

The first steps to applying for a position in the U.S. involve contacting the Canadian Resident Matching Service (CaRMS) and obtaining an identification number, known as a token. Using the token, students will be able to login to the Electronic Residency Application Service (ERAS). CaRMS acts as the Dean's Office, and processes the application documents. These include academic transcripts, letters of recommendation, Dean's letter, USMLE results, personal statement, and photograph. These are made available by CaRMS to the ERAS web-based Post Office. Designated residency programs will be able to download the information from the ERAS website. Students also need to register with the National Resident Matching Program to participate in the U.S. Match. For more information, visit: www.aamc.org/students/eras and www.nrmp.org. Unless Canadian candidates also possess a U.S. Green Card or American citizenship, they will need to obtain a work visa before being allowed to pursue clinical training. Not all hospitals sponsor candidates for work visas. Check with individual programs to determine their policies.

Important Note for Applicants Enrolled in Both the U.S. and Canadian Residency Match:

While students can register for NRMP and CaRMS simultaneously, they should be aware that they cannot reserve residency spots in both countries. They should make note of which Match occurs first, as they will be required to withdraw the pending application from the other country once matched to a program.

Final Thoughts

Canadian medical schools provide an education comparable to the top tier schools in the U.S. The qualities needed to be competitive for medical school are identical in both countries. Canadian provincial residents get priority for admission at most schools, but there are some universities in Eastern Canada which consider international students. The years of training required for specialties can differ from the U.S. Students interested in studying in one country and working in another should check with State and Provincial Boards to determine criteria for licensure in their intended specialty. For more information on Canadian medical schools, refer to Appendix C.

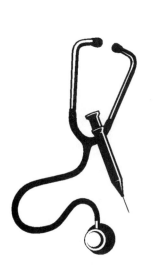

Part 4: Doctor in Training

Introduction to Part Four:

By now, you've learnt about how to get into medical school. You know how to maximize your chances of admission, and how to prepare a stellar application. You may feel ready to make your move into the world of medicine, but there's still an important piece missing. What is it like to be a medical student? Is studying medicine different from any other educational program? The truth is that the culture of medical education deserves special attention. Part 4 takes you into the life of a busy medical student. It describes the curriculum of the four years of medical school, and takes you through the landmark experiences - from cadaver dissection in the anatomy lab to being part of a code blue for a patient in cardiac arrest. It details the Board Exams that students are expected to take during medical school and residency. Sections on each of the core rotations in medicine are described through the eyes of a medical student, as she struggles to understand her role as a doctor in training. Becoming a physician is more than just receiving a formal education. It will change you profoundly as you go through the steps, and that will be just the beginning.

Chapter 11: Pre-Clinical Years: From Cadavers to Live Humans

"Welcome to medical school. Half of the knowledge you gain here
will be outdated in the next five years..."
- Dean of Admission's address to my medical school class

The first two years of medical school, known as the pre-clinical years, are spent learning about the functions of the human body, diseases and the medical interventions that can prolong good health - fundamental principles necessary to the practice of medicine. Medical students sit in dark lecture theatres, bone-chilling cold anatomy labs and small classrooms filled with body specimens in jars trying to learn the minutiae of health and disease. At this point, students spend the majority of their time with books and cadavers rather than real patients. The privilege of being a doctor to a patient must wait until a student has successfully completed the first two years of intense studying and passed rigorous school and Board exams.

The medical world speaks a language of its own, and one of the most important tasks of the first two years will be to master its gigantic vocabulary. The number of new terms that students learn in the first year alone is estimated to be around ten thousand, most with their origins in Latin and Greek.

Students should not expect to come away from the first two years thinking that they have learnt all there is to know about medicine. These foundation years teach enough that the basic principles can be understood once you begin working with patients. More than the exposure to basic medicine, the real value of the pre-clinical years is the exposure to a world from which most people are sheltered.

You will meet drug addicts, recovering alcoholics, schizophrenic patients, patients living with debilitating conditions and children with cancer. They will speak to you about their lives and struggles and try to make you see the world through their eyes. Their goal is to instill a sense of compassion and understanding before you start on the medical wards.

For many students, the first two years can be a struggle due to the overwhelming volume of information presented. Medical science knowledge, which continues to grow and change rapidly, will be crammed into these two short years. The direct relevance of the material to patient care can be difficult to comprehend at times. For example, does the Krebs cycle really affect how you will manage Mrs. Smith's diabetes? The short answer is yes. Doctors are more than just bedside clinicians. They can also choose to be scientists. Many doctors are actively involved in research, and the basic components of biology and physiology form the core of their work. Many post-graduate programs like Internal Medicine require a research project before qualifying doctors for independent practice. So while memorizing the biochemical pathways can feel like a waste of precious brain space at this point, it does serve a purpose beyond just being exam material.

Medical School Curriculums

Different learning methods are used by medical schools to achieve the same purpose. The older and traditional method of teaching focuses mainly on the basic Sciences in the first two years. Students attend up to six hours of lectures a day, on topics such as Physiology, Biochemistry and Embryology, with Gross Anatomy and Histology labs interspersed in the curriculum. Students tend to be used to this type of teaching from their undergraduate years, where a lecturer teaches from a podium and students scribble down notes. Relevance to patients and the practice of medicine can be harder to grasp with this approach.

Today, more schools are turning towards a problem-based curriculum (PBL), which integrates basic sciences with clinical medicine from the first day. In PBL, students focus on a clinical problem each week, and work towards uncovering its science components. They discuss the case's histological, pathological, clinical and pharmacological aspects.

PBL takes place in small groups, and is combined with time for independent study. Students are divided into groups of around six to eight students, and a faculty member leads the discussion at each meeting. Students are presented with a scenario about a patient, and encouraged to do their own research to find the information that is relevant to solving the problem. The main subjects covered in this manner include Infectious Diseases, Hematology (blood), Oncology (cancer),

Cardiovascular (heart), Pulmonary (lungs), Renal (kidneys), Gastrointestinal (digestive organs), Growth and Development, Brain and Spinal Cord, Behavioral Science and Reproduction. Advantages of PBL are its student-oriented approach, emphasis on independent learning, and direct relevance to patient care. Lab sessions, and a minimum number of lectures continue to be an important part of the curriculum, and serve as a means of enhancing the learning taking place in small groups. Early exposure to patients is also an integral part of this method. Students might be required to spend a set number of hours per week with a medical doctor starting from the first year. Some schools invite patients to forums to speak to students about their experiences in dealing with illness.

The following example illustrates a typical scenario given to students as part of problem-based learning. The case lasts for one week, with students meeting in small groups up to three times over the week to discuss their findings and to be given more information about the case. At the end of the week, the solution is provided, with an opportunity to discuss any remaining issues in greater depth with an expert.

Problem-based Learning Case Scenario:

Todd Horner is a 68 year old man who presents to his family doctor's office with complaints of increased shortness of breath over the past two weeks. His medical history is relevant for high blood pressure and cancer of the prostate. He had a prostatectomy (surgical removal of the prostate) five years ago.

Students get a short history of the problem in the first session. As a group, they need to address what other information is necessary to know. This might include more information about the shortness of breath, such as when the patient experiences it, as well as any other associated symptoms. Students make a list of the possible causes of shortness of breath. During the session, they discover that they need to access other resources to find out how the patient's past medical history may be contributing to his current problems. They then make a list of the learning issues, with a plan to return with the answers.

At the next session, more is learnt about the patient.

Mr. Horner also complains of swollen legs and says that his wife feels he has gained a lot of weight recently. He has tried to cut down on his smoking, and now smokes only 2 packs a day, but it hasn't helped. His father died of a heart attack at age 61 and his mother died of breast cancer at age 59. Mr. Horner wants to know the reason for the shortness of breath, and what can be done to treat the problem.

By now, students have collected information on all likely causes of shortness of breath. They use the additional information to narrow the list down to the most likely cause. Weight gain and swollen legs may indicate congestive heart failure. The history of smoking puts him at risk for lung cancer. Learning issues for the day include further information on the mechanisms of heart and lung disease, the best diagnostic tests and effective treatments.

During the last session, students review the information collected over the week to arrive at a better understanding of cardiac and pulmonary function, symptoms and causes of heart failure and lung cancer, diagnostic tools, and treatments for these conditions. They discuss information on survival rates, and complications of treatment.

In addition to the PBL sessions and standard lectures on Physiology, Pharmacology, Biochemistry and Microbiology, students will be required to take Gross Anatomy, Histology, Neurosciences, Clinical Skills, and Medical Ethics during the pre-clinical years. The following sections describe these courses.

Gross Anatomy

There are many new innovations in medical teaching, but Gross Anatomy has been taught in much the same way since the days of Hippocrates. The experience in this course is bound to leave a permanent imprint in your life. It is the medical student's first initiation into a profession where society sanctions actions that are denied to everybody else. When done for the purposes of knowledge, it is called dissecting a cadaver. If done by anyone else, it would be termed disfiguring a corpse, and lead to criminal prosecution.

I must admit that I was initially baffled as to why the course was called Gross Anatomy. Surely, the word gross wasn't meant to imply disgust, was it? I later learnt that 'gross' meant 'large' or 'visible to the eye'.

Students approach the first session of Gross Anatomy with a mixture of curiosity and trepidation. Those who know they are prone to lightheadedness are the most uncomfortable. It is largely up to the Anatomy instructor on how the first exposure is handled.

My class was fortunate to have a thoughtful professor who met with us in the lecture theatre before heading to the first Gross Anatomy session. He explained the responsibility entrusted on us by all those we were to meet in the lab. He read out a letter written by a donor that eloquently explained the donor's reasons for choosing to gift his body to medical students. Lastly, he explained that the first dissection would start with the hand. As he spoke, he uncovered a small portion of a dissected arm from under a thick yellow cloth. His movements were very slow and deliberate as he pointed to the muscles, nerves and blood vessels that we would encounter in our first dissection that day.

The Anatomy lab has its own set of strict rules, and the Anatomy instructor will lay these out before students step into the lab. Violating these rules is one of the grounds for being disciplined, and even expelled from medical school.

Rules in the Gross Anatomy Lab
1. Always behave respectfully around the cadavers
2. No photographs allowed of the cadavers or of each other in the lab
3. Always wear a lab coat
4. No food or drinks
5. No open toed shoes

Students will be asked to name their cadaver on their first day in the lab. Four to eight students are assigned to work on one body during the year, so it will be a group decision. Since the cadaver's head remains securely covered with a cloth bag until later in the year, his or her looks cannot be relied upon to pick the right name. Naming the cadaver is a ritual, but it also reinforces that the body used to belong to a real person. Students aren't given any information on the history of the cadaver. They will never find out the real name, age, medical history or cause of death. Dissecting a cadaver is vastly different from performing surgery on a live body. A cadaver's skin is cold and leathery, and blood never obscures the area being cut as it has been drained.

My Gross Anatomy dissection group decided to name our cadaver 'Mort'. It was a play on words. In French, mort means deceased.

The dress code for Anatomy lab mandates a long white lab coat and closed shoes. The scalpels used for dissection are very sharp, and can easily fall from unskilled hands onto unprotected toes. This policy on closed shoes applies in hospitals as well.

The cadavers are kept individually in metal boxes on top of stainless steel tables. The lab is usually stark white, tiled, and maintained at a cold temperature. The cadavers have been preserved, and the smell of the preservative permeates every inch of the lab. By the end of the first session, it will have found its way into the student's clothes, hair and skin. Most students keep two anatomy books. One is used for studying at home, and the second is used in the lab for quick reference during the dissections. In addition to taking on the smell of the lab, the book often ends up with flecks of skin and muscle on it. It is best kept in the lab. Lockers are provided for the storage of lab coats, clothes, books and dissection kit.

As part of the Gross Anatomy course, students are also given a bag of bones and skull to take home for study. These are actual human bones, and tremendously useful for learning names, shapes and muscle attachments.

It is rare for an individual not to be moved by the experience of dissecting a cadaver in some way. On a personal level, the intimate confrontation with death left me emotionally drained. I didn't react outwardly while in the lab, but was overwhelmed by tears later that evening.

Despite the initial jitters, students do get accustomed to the lab within a short period of time. The course becomes very relevant once students begin the clinical rotations. It will allow students to visualize the anatomy clearly in their mind's eye as they examine patients, assist in surgeries and look at X-rays, CT scans and MRIs.

Anatomy lab sessions are organized around specific body systems. For example, the upper extremities, or arms, might be dissected in the first month. The next system would be the thorax, or chest cavity, followed by abdomen, pelvis, lower extremities (legs) and face. Students are tested on written exams and lab exams. In a typical lab exam, the instructor will indicate a muscle, nerve, blood vessel, bone or anatomic landmark and ask for its name. Usually, the dissected body part looks quite different from the colorful drawings in anatomy books, so spending long hours in the lab prior to the exam are a must.

Histology Lab

Histology represents the other end of the spectrum when studying the human body. It is a study of the body and its functions, but at the microscopic level of the cell. Students will be loaned a microscope, or required to rent one. They don't need to have any previous experience using a microscope. Some students can only tolerate using the microscope for a couple of hours at a time, as it is known to bring on a formidable headache from the focusing and concentration efforts required.

Similar to Anatomy, the course is organized around body systems. Pre-prepared slides will be available for study, and will contain sections of tissue taken from all parts of the body. The student will spend many hours in front of the microscope in an aim is to identify the sections based on the appearance. For example, if the week's topic is endocrinology (the study of secretion of endocrine glands which produce an effect elsewhere in the body), the slides would be of the thyroid gland in the neck, the pituitary gland in the brain, the pancreas which secretes insulin, and the adrenal glands above the kidneys.

The study of Histology in medical school has led to some students finding their passion for Pathology. Pathologists are specialists who identify diseases, such as cancer, by studying cells and tissues under a microscope.

Weekly lectures supplement the lab work. Students are provided with images from electron microscopes, which provide greater magnification than possible with the standard microscope. During the Histology exam, the instructor places a number of slides on an overhead projector, and asks students to name the organ or function of the tissue.

Neurosciences

The Neurosciences portion of the curriculum will feel like you are studying Neurology, Psychiatry and Neurosurgery at the same time. In Neurosciences, students study the anatomy and function of the brain and spinal cord. This course is one of the most intense blocks in the first two years of the medical school curriculum, due to the tremendous amount of minute details that need to be learned. It is imperative to keep up with the material in this course in order to pass the exam.

The brain is a very delicate and sophisticated organ. In appearance, it is quite similar to a cauliflower that has turned brown. Dissection is usually done only by the instructor, and students are provided specimens of brain that have already been expertly dissected to show the relevant parts.

Lectures and histology sessions supplement this course, so students are able to integrate the structure of the brain with clinically relevant information. For example, when discussing the ability for language, students will be able to see the exact areas of the brain responsible for speech. For most people, particularly those who are right-handed, speech is controlled by the left side of the brain. One part, known as Broca's area, controls speech production, and another, known as Wernicke's area, controls the ability to understand language. In lectures, instructors will discuss what happens if these parts of the brain are affected by diseases such as strokes or tumors. If Broca's area is affected, patients can still understand language and know what they wish to say, but aren't able to communicate with fluent speech. The sounds they create aren't easily understood, leaving the patient feeling tremendously frustrated. Since Broca's area is situated close to the region where arm and leg movements are controlled, patients may also have right-sided weakness or paralysis. When Wernicke's area is affected, patients don't have difficulty producing sound, but their sentences have little meaning as they choose the wrong words or invent new sounds. Interestingly, in these cases, the patients do not recognize that their speech is incomprehensible to everyone else, and don't experience the same level of frustration as a patient with Broca's deficit.

Lectures on human behavior are equally fascinating, and will force students to look deeper into their own personalities. Students can and often do fall into the trap of thinking that the diseases they are studying are directly applicable to them. This is known as the 'medical student syndrome' and is a mild form of hypochondria. The concerns are usually about a cancer or a neurological problem, and can generate a lot of anxiety. However, the fear that they might have a brain tumor because of that headache last week is quickly replaced by the fear of something else just as disastrous once the lecture topic changes. It doesn't persist for long.

Clinical Skills

Many medical schools have changed their traditional curriculums to one that provides early exposure to patients. The Clinical Skills course allows medical students to learn history taking and physical exam skills on volunteer patients. Medical students meet with an instructor and patients on a regular schedule during the first two years. The clinical skills course uses a systems-based approach, so one month might cover the cardiovascular system, the next covers the pulmonary system, and so forth.

A Typical Clinical Skills Session:

For a week that covers the subject of liver, the volunteer patient might present with a history of hepatitis (inflammation of the liver). Students first ask focused questions relevant to the abdominal system, such as the presence of pain and color of stools and urine. The remainder of the session is spent learning how to examine a liver. This includes techniques such as inspecting the patient's eyes, hands, chest and abdomen for clues about the presence of liver disease. Telltale signs are yellowing of the skin and visible blood vessels on the chest wall. Then, students are taught how to percuss (identify the liver by tapping on the skin) and palpate (feel for the size, consistency and any abnormalities).

Some medical schools also offer students the opportunity to work with doctors and patients from the first year. This takes place in outpatient clinics. One to two students are paired with a doctor, and they see patients together. In the early stages, students merely observe. As they gain confidence, they begin seeing patients independently for the first few minutes to obtain information on the reason for the patient's visit. Most doctors will permit students to write in the patient's chart. As their experience increases, students will begin taking the relevant vital signs, such as blood pressure and pulse, and examining the patients. Some doctors like students to formulate a diagnosis and management plan also.

On the first day of our session with a Family Practice doctor, my medical student partner and I were told to practice taking each other's blood pressure. Left alone in the examination room, we soon realized that neither one of us knew what to do with the sphygmomanometer hanging on the wall. We managed to place the blood pressure cuff correctly, but then looked helplessly at the brand-new stethoscopes hanging around our necks. The doctor taught us the correct procedure later, with a grin on his face that wouldn't go away.

The majority of patients are tolerant of Student Doctors. They enjoy the extra attention, and like being part of the teaching process. The very basic skills needed in a good doctor are learnt with these patients: the art of communication, examining patients, learning to write prescriptions, giving injections, maintaining a patient's chart, interpreting lab results, performing pap smears, using a Doppler ultrasound to find the heart beat of a fetus, learning how to hold a child to perform an ear exam, counseling patients on smoking and weight control, among many others.

Medical Ethics

One of the most important changes that have occurred in medical school curriculums is the emphasis on ethics and social awareness. Future doctors are being taught about ethical principles to help guide them in this age where technology has enabled progress, but the issue of whether it is always appropriate to proceed just because it is possible isn't clearly answered. Some principles have their roots buried deep in the history of medicine. Hippocrates said "Declare the past, diagnose the present, foretell the future; practice these acts. As to diseases, make a habit of two things-to help, or at least to do no harm." To help is now known as the principle of beneficence, and to do no harm as the principle of non-maleficence. Another important guiding principle is autonomy. The emphasis on autonomy is a change from the paternalistic days of medicine when doctors routinely made decisions on behalf of the patient. Today's medicine demands that patients be presented with all their options, and that the final decision regarding their medical lives rest with them.

Doctors deal with questions of ethics daily in their practices. Consider the following situation that I encountered in the hospital: Family members requested that their mother not be told about her diagnosis of breast cancer, as they feared it would break her spirit. They suggested telling her that her chemotherapy medications were vitamins. What is the ethically correct action in this case? What are the doctor's duties to her patient?

Getting a Head-Start on your Future

Students will have more personal time for work and fun in the first two years than in the last two. They will also have a two to three month vacation between the first and second year. Plan to use your extra time wisely. It can be spent working at a part time job or doing research in a field of interest. While the thought of doing more work when all you want is a vacation sounds like a terrible idea, there are ways of using the time to your greatest advantage.

Students who plan to pursue competitive post-graduate positions after medical school will gain a distinct advantage by doing research during the summers. Clinical researchers can be found within the Faculty of Medicine, or students can consider approaching respected experts at other medical schools as well. Students can negotiate spending a portion of their summers on the research project, and then take the rest of the time for some personal relaxation.

Another good option for the summer is to volunteer at a local Emergency Department or in a General Physician's office. If there is a choice between these two, choose the E.R. It is the best place to learn medicine in a short time frame. The constant turnover of patients will provide exposure to all types of illnesses. It is also the ideal environment to learn basic medical student skills like suturing, placing intravenous lines and drawing blood. One month of Emergency Room experience is adequate to prepare you for the clinical years, and the rest of the summer can be spent sitting on a beach in Hawaii.

Right before the first two years draw to a close, students face Step 1 of the United States Medical Licensing Exams (USMLE). Increasingly, medical schools are requiring students to pass this exam to advance to the clinical years. Step 1 tests the student's knowledge about the basic sciences and organ systems, including normal and diseased states. The subject areas tested include: Anatomy, Behavioral Sciences, Biochemistry, Microbiology, Molecular and Cell Biology, Pathology, Pharmacology, Physiology, Genetics, Aging, Immunology and Nutrition.

The score obtained on the Step 1 may play a role when applying for a residency position. Some Residency Directors look at the scores of the Step 1 and Step 2 (taken during the fourth year) to choose amongst competitive candidates. Step 3 is written during post-graduate residency training.

Final Thoughts

The first two years of medical school can be best described as awe-inspiring and challenging. Sometimes exhilarating but also frustrating. Your eyes will be opened to a vastly different world. You will discover a number of truths about yourself during this time. One of the most important may be your ability to handle stress. This is the appropriate time to pay attention to the aphorism 'Doctor, first heal thyself'. Students who are having difficulty dealing with studies or their emotions are strongly encouraged to seek help. Studies estimate that up to a third of medical students are clinically depressed. Medical professionals have a higher than average rate of suicide, and may turn to narcotic and alcohol abuse as ways of coping. Identifying stressors and seeking help early is crucial. Students need to be able to function at their best - physically and emotionally- as they begin their next phase of training.

Chapter 12: Clinical Years

"The life so short, the craft so long to learn" - Hippocrates

Successful completion of the first two years of medical school allows the student to proceed to the next phase of learning: real life in a hospital. The third and fourth years of medical school take place on hospital wards, clinics, the Emergency Room, and are called the clinical years. This is the first time that medical students are fully immersed in the hospital environment and in patient's lives.

On entering the third year, students are given a schedule that outlines their next twelve months. The schedule lists all the rotations that medical students are required to successfully complete to advance to the fourth year. These core rotations are: Emergency Medicine, General Surgery, Internal Medicine, Obstetrics, Gynecology, Pediatrics, Psychiatry and Family Practice. Some schools also require Neurology, Ophthalmology, Anesthesiology, Radiology, and Orthopedic Surgery. Each rotation lasts from 4 weeks to 12 weeks, with emphasis on fields with broad scopes, such as Internal Medicine, Family Practice, General Surgery and Pediatrics.

The anxiety at this critical phase of learning can be overwhelming. It presents a tremendous learning curve educationally. While students have a large databank of information by this point, they still don't know how to make the leap from book knowledge to helping a real patient. Students tend to put a lot of unrealistic expectations on themselves at this stage. Part of this has to do with their fear of mistaking mistakes and unintentionally harming patients, as well as the discomfort of not knowing how to handle the smallest tasks in a hospital.

Ordering a pain-reliever for a patient during my first rotation had me panicked. I consulted two texts and checked with the resident to make sure that I was prescribing the common over-the-counter headache medication appropriately.

Medical students are accustomed to being among the top few percent in any academic endeavor. It takes a lot of humility to realize that they will be regarded as nothing more than as liabilities to the hospital culture during the first few months of training, while they gain the skills needed to be of value to patients.

The hospital structure also requires adjustment for the student. There is a definite hierarchy that exists in a training institution, and medical students land at the bottom of the heap. The Attending Physicians hold the ultimate responsibility for the patients. These are doctors who have completed their training as residents in a particular field, allowing them to practice independently. Below the Attending Physician is the Chief Resident. A Chief Resident is a physician in the final year of training, and has taken on hospital administrative responsibilities in addition to completing the residency requirements. Then come the Senior Residents, followed by Junior Residents, and interns. Interns are residents in their first year of training. Trailing the end are the senior medical students (fourth year students known as sub-interns), and, finally, the junior medical students (third year students).

Medical students are assigned to work directly under the supervision of interns or residents. They aren't allowed to order tests, medications or write notes in a patient chart without a co-signature from an MD

The practicalities of completing simple tasks are initially a struggle for the student. For example, the first few weeks are spent mastering the art of venipuncture, or drawing blood. The procedure is relatively simple. It requires a tourniquet (tight band) to be put around the patient's upper arm to slow down the flow of blood from the arm veins back to the heart. Once the veins plump up with blood, the student applies an alcohol swab to sterilize the area, and then inserts a needle into the vein. If the needle has successfully entered the vein, the student is rewarded with a quick flow of blood into the glass tube attached to the needle. Students also learn how to place intravenous lines and take arterial blood gas samples in the first few weeks.

You will find many believers of superstition among on-call doctors. One of the first things a medical student learns from a resident is never to say the word 'quiet', as in 'Why is it so quiet today?' It tempts fate to prove you wrong. Many will also insist that a full moon makes the E.R. a madhouse, but studies don't substantiate such beliefs.

The techniques aren't complicated, but the anxiety of being around needles and blood, and worries of accidently injuring yourself, make the first few attempts a challenge. In an age where HIV and Hepatitis B and C are common in hospitals, even simple procedures should never be taken lightly. One small slip that leads to a needlestick injury will require students to take multiple blood tests over a period of weeks to months to check if they have contracted the virus. In addition, they will need to start taking medications such as anti-retroviral drugs used to treat HIV positive patients until it can be verified that the HIV virus hasn't been transmitted to them.

In the operating room, students are often viewed as hazards to the sterility of the surgery, and are watched vigilantly by the surgeon and surgical nurses. This is for good reason, as medical students often don't know what to do with their restless gloved hands, and usually end up touching an unsterile field. If this hand later touches any part of the surgical environment, the patient is at risk of getting an infection. Some surgeons have been known to ask medical students to leave the operating room if they make such mistakes during the surgery.

The third year clinical rotations can be a rude awakening for the idealistic medical student. While the first two years took place in a protected academic environment, the culture in the hospital demands a 'sink or swim' attitude. The history of medical training is rampant with stories of Attending Physicians and residents who dehumanize medicine for students by constantly demoralizing, criticizing and acting as poor examples of the humanitarian doctor that we have idealized in our imaginations. Since medical training necessitates an apprentice-teacher model in the hospital, one of the biggest challenges of the clinical years is to avoid being negatively affected by inconsiderate superiors.

Despite the challenges, these clinical years build the framework for a future confident doctor. The third year is filled with many firsts - the first baby delivery, the first correct diagnosis of heart failure, appendicitis, stroke, the first chance to participate in a surgery, the first opportunity to perform CPR to save a real life. It is also the case that the things students aren't taught are the ones that make the journey memorable. Such as learning to sit with a patient who has just been diagnosed with cancer, or getting a smile from a 3 year old patient who had only previously cried at the sight of you.

Each student develops into a doctor at his or her own pace. The practical experiences gained in the clinical years are precious, as are the lessons that each patient teaches you. Perhaps there is no better way to illustrate the process than to have you walk alongside the steps of one medical student. The experiences are my own, but the lessons echo those of countless medical students. For anyone thinking seriously of a medical career, these accounts will provide a glimpse of the life that new doctors face.

Emergency Medicine

The Emergency Room is a part of the hospital that everyone has seen at some point. Whether it was for a broken bone, or a vigil in the waiting room for news about a family member, we are familiar with the function of such a place. Patients come seeking urgent treatment at all hours. An E.R. becomes a meeting place of society, striving to serve everybody.

Emergency Medicine is one of the rare fields that don't require medical students to take on-call duties. Students work in day or night shifts of up to 12 hours, five days a week. For the novice medical student, it is exhilarating as well as a little frightening. The pace can be hectic, so much so that sometimes hospitals are forced to close their doors and divert ambulances to other hospitals.

The E.R. physician must have the skills to accurately recognize symptoms and initiate early treatment. They never know what to expect from the next patient who walks in through the door. It might be a patient requiring stitches from being in a bar fight, or a patient with a sudden loss of vision because of retinal detachment. They need diverse skills and superb medical knowledge to do their jobs well. It is not easy to distinguish between a patient suffering a heart attack, and one experiencing a bad case of heartburn from the patient's story alone, and it takes a detective's persistence to find the true cause of chest pain in such patients. Now put a medical student with minimal clinical experience in this environment. The medical school had assigned the Emergency Room as my first rotation. I found out my schedule during the summer, a month prior to starting the rotation. I didn't sleep well that whole month in anticipation of my first day.

Progress Notes

I showed up half an hour early for my night shift in the E.R. I was self-conscious about my starched, snow-white short lab jacket, worn only by medical students in the hospital. It must have boldly declared 'Watch Out. Amateur on the Floor!" Even if patients missed that, I am sure they could have smelled my uncertainty. And if they missed that also, the pools of sweat on the floor would have been fair warning.

Unlike the rest of the hospital, lights in the E.R. are glaringly bright, and the noise never stops. Cardiac monitors and IV machines continuously beep in the background. Traffic flows into the E.R. bay at all hours. I was sure that the E.R. couldn't possibly provide a quiet environment conducive to clear thinking.

My supervising physician for the night was Dr. Gabriel. I found him easily enough by his long white jacket. Clearly a man of few words, he nodded at me when I introduced myself, and pointed me towards the new charts. He told me to start seeing patients, and once I had done the history and physical exams, I was to find him again to go over the treatment plan.

Wait, I thought. Wasn't he going to ease me into the process by showing me how it is done first? This is my first day in the hospital! These patients are sick! My experience in the last two years had been limited to standardized patients, or actors pretending to have physical complaints. Real patients had been limited to those in the clinic, most of whom had chronic and non-life-threatening conditions. I had yet to deal with an acutely sick patient.

Mustering up some courage, I picked up the chart next in queue. Mr. Donald.

I found my first patient sitting up in bed, dressed in pale blue hospital pajamas. He was a slim, white male, and didn't look very sick at all. This comforted me. I introduced myself as a medical student, and paused for a brief second to see if my title unnerved him. I had heard from senior classmates that some patients refused to be seen by students. But Mr. Donald just nodded. Pleased, I continued. What had led him to the hospital today? The triage nurse had written 'hematuria' on his chart. Bloody urine.

It started this morning, he explained. It was bright red. No, there was no pain. He was in good health otherwise. There were no other symptoms. I touched his abdomen delicately. Deeper, the voice inside my head said. Are you afraid he's going to run away? Do a better exam! I slowly dug my hand into his soft belly. Not even a wince. I lightly tapped over his bladder with one gloved finger over another. It didn't seem enlarged. His genitalia appeared normal. I moved my stethoscope over his lungs and heart and listened carefully. It sounded just like my own organs. I thanked him and told him I would return shortly.

"Is it something serious, doctor?" he asked as I prepared to leave.

My chest must have swelled with pride when he addressed me as doctor. I was actually taking care of a patient! I was his doctor! He wanted my opinion! Was I allowed to hug a patient?

"Um, we can't be sure yet, Mr. Donald. Let's check your urine first. Perhaps we'll need to send you for further tests. Then we'll know more." That sounded professional, didn't it? In the first year of medical school, a Family Practice doctor had given me some advice: *Patients will tell you the most intimate details of their lives, things that they sometimes keep from their spouses and children. As a doctor, your duty is to act professionally towards your patients. Being professional is nothing more than acting - going through the motions - every single day until it becomes second nature to you.*

As I sat at the nursing station, writing up my findings, my mind thought of possibilities for Mr. Donald's condition. Cancer? Infection? A large prostrate? A kidney stone? Could sexually transmitted diseases cause red urine? I couldn't recall with certainty at that moment.

A nurse left his room with a small plastic container, and I followed her into the utilities room. The urine was certainly red. She told me that she was sending it to the lab, and we would know the results within an hour.

Immensely pleased with myself, I set off to find the Attending. He was on the side of the E.R. reserved for more critical patients. Heart attacks, trauma victims, brain bleeds. I was walking past the entrance of the ambulance bay when the doors suddenly flung open, forcing me to jump aside to avoid being hit. Two EMT's rushed in with a gurney, and a third sat on top performing CPR on a half-naked body. I followed the action into the main E.R..

A swarm of nurses seemed to appear at the same time in the trauma area. "What's the story?" someone called out. The patient was tall and obese. His abdomen flopped on both sides of the gurney. He wasn't wearing a shirt, and his pants were in the process of being cut off. One nurse was taking his blood pressure, another was trying to attach cardiac leads even as the paramedic continued to perform CPR on the patient's chest. The patient had a breathing tube sticking out of his mouth, and I assumed that it had been put in by the EMT's in the field. A third nurse now stood at the head of the bed pushing air into the patient's lungs through an inflated bag.

"51 year old male, found unresponsive in a parking lot. Witnesses say he collapsed as he was walking out of a bank. Glasgow coma scale of 3. History is unclear. He's been down for fifteen minutes now."

I knew that the Glasgow Coma Scale measured a person's level of consciousness. A score of 3 was the lowest number on the scale, and meant that the patient had no response, even to pain. A team of ten people now stood surrounding the patient, including myself. I felt a hand on my elbow. Dr. Gabriel's lanky form had appeared beside me. He asked if I had performed CPR before. "Yes, I know CPR," I quickly replied. I had practiced it on a dummy during the training course.

At Dr. Gabriel's instructions, the EMT jumped down from the gurney and someone passed gloves into my hands. A small stool had materialized for me to stand on. I climbed up and leaned over the patient, one hand placed on top of the other, elbows locked. I landmarked the heels of my hands over the bottom of his breast bone, and started compressing. In and out. In and out. A hundred times a minute, just as I had been taught a month ago at the CPR class.

"I can't get a blood pressure," a voice called out.

"There's no pulse."

"Where's the central line kit?"

My face was just inches over the patient's. He appeared ashen, and his lips had turned a light shade of blue. I struggled to continue compressions. His chest wasn't as pliant as the dummy's. There was actual muscle and bones underneath my hands. I had heard that ribs often cracked during CPR, particularly those of elderly patients. I felt sweat dripping down my forehead. My stethoscope slid off my neck onto the floor. I wished I had taken my white jacket off. The weight of all the handbooks and metallic instruments in my pockets was starting to strain my shoulders.

"Stop compressions....stop compressions!" A nurse firmly put her hand over mine, and I realized that Dr. Gabriel's order was being directed towards me. I stepped down, and an EKG tracing was obtained. Even I could recognize a flat line.

"Thank you all. We are stopping the code." The Attending's eyes flicked towards the clock. "Time of death 10:17 p.m."

What?

It took only seconds for the trauma bay to empty out. Ten pairs of gloves were tossed into the garbage, and nursing aides entered to clean the area. I still didn't understand what had happened. That had seemed so short. More than five minutes couldn't have elapsed. Surely codes went on longer than that, even on the TV medical dramas! Shouldn't we have kept trying until a cardiac rhythm was obtained? Couldn't we shock his heart back with paddles? Couldn't we cut open his chest and massage his heart? I peered into the eyes of our unknown patient. His pupils appeared as large plates against the pale grey iris. I was used to the wrinkled cold skin of cadavers in the anatomy lab, but his was still smooth. How long would it take to develop that same rough texture?

Dr. Gabriel waved me over to the sitting area. He was filling out the death certificate. "How's your patient?" he asked, without lifting his head from the forms.

The dead one? No, of course not.

"He's got hematuria." *Why didn't we work harder on our last patient, Dr. Gabriel?*

"What does his urine show?"

"It's visibly red, but the lab results are not back yet." *Why did you stop the code?!*

Should I just ask him? Or was it a naïve question? There was a long line of patients waiting to be seen. I would only be slowing down the pace. Besides, nobody else had seemed very concerned.

"We'll see him once his results are back. If he has bled a lot, we should check his blood count also. But we'll order the workup once we've see him together. Do you want to see another patient?"

"Um, yeah. I guess so." Perhaps it was my voice, or that I stood a second too long without reaching for another chart. "Do you have a question?" he asked.

"Uh, yeah. What happens now to this patient? I mean, what are you going to tell his family?"

"I'll tell them that he had a cardiac arrest, likely secondary to a myocardial infarction. An autopsy will be able to tell us better." He continued to fill out the forms. "I'll tell them that we attempted to resuscitate him, but it was futile."

So our patient had most likely died of a heart attack.

"Do codes always last only 5 minutes?" I knew that my inexperience showed with that question, but I would be haunted for the rest of the night if I didn't ask.

Dr. Gabriel took off his glasses, shuffled the papers and handed them to the desk clerk. "No. This patient was already dead before we started working on him. He should never have been brought to the hospital. Do you know how long brains are viable without oxygen?"

Yes, I did. 4 minutes.

"The paramedics had already worked on him for fifteen minutes. He had no pulse, no blood pressure, and no cardiac rhythm. No matter how hard we try, we're still not at the point where we can breathe life back into a dead person."

He handed me a new chart, and left with a new one himself. I went back to the trauma bay, and peered through the glass doors. The nursing aides had laid out clean sheets over the patient's body, and there was even a pillow beneath his head. The breathing tube was gone. All the wires had been disconnected. His eyes were closed, and he finally looked peaceful. I realized later that I never found out his name.

My shoulders hurt from the CPR. I stopped to check on Mr. Donald. His results were back, and I was taken by surprise. There was no trace of blood in his urine. I went to see him, and asked if he could provide another sample of urine. This one I would test myself with a strip.

Again, his urine was red, but the dipstick didn't show any signs of blood either.

"Well, what do you think it is?" Dr. Gabriel later questioned. We were sitting at the nursing station reviewing the night's cases.

I shook my head. "I don't know." This was my first diagnostic failure. Had I known of the numerous others that would come later, maybe I wouldn't have felt so defeated.

"Beets," Dr. Gabriel said. "He says that he ate more than a dozen red beets last night."

Nobody had warned me about beets.

One of my many heavy pocketbooks later confirmed that red urine without any signs of blood can be due to a food dye, fresh beets, medications and a few other diagnoses that didn't fit the clinical picture.

Further tests confirmed that Mr. Donald really did not have any evidence of a serious affliction other than his passion for the red vegetable. We discharged him home at two in the morning.

As the night wore on, the waiting room started looking emptier. I learnt how to suture lacerations on two patients, and watched the Surgical Trauma Team in action as daybreak arose. Two gunshot victims were brought in, and one was rushed to surgery immediately. The second was stable, but X-rays showed that he had a bullet lodged in his left buttock. He kept insisting loudly of his innocence, especially when the police officers outside the trauma bay drifted within hearing distance.

I would see more gunshot victims throughout the month, and there was one phrase that became comical from being heard over and over again: "I was just walking on the street minding my own business when I got shot." One could almost believe that minding one's own business was the highest risk factor for catching a bullet.

In retrospect, the E.R. provided ample opportunity to see a full range of acute problems. My confidence grew slowly during the month, but I also realized how much there was left to learn. Knowing biochemical pathways and making histological diagnoses seemed irrelevant here. I would need to shift focus to recognizing common presentations of illnesses. Attendings are fond of saying: When you hear hoofbeats, think horses, not zebras. Zebras are the rare, exciting cases in medicine that medical students think of first, but seldom encounter. The difficult part was to relegate the zebras to the bottom of my differential diagnosis list when seeing patients. Hippocrates said it best over 2500 years ago: "Life is short, the art long, opportunity fleeting, experiment treacherous, judgment difficult."

General Surgery

It wasn't until my second rotation that I realized what a General Surgeon does. As I found out, General Surgeons are not trained to perform all surgeries, as their title suggests. They deal with specific areas, mainly with the abdomen and its organs for conditions such as appendicitis, bowel obstructions and colon cancers. They also perform breast biopsies and mastectomies for breast cancer.

Medical students interested in any type of surgery look forward to this rotation as it gives the first opportunity to assist in real surgeries. For students who realize that the scalpel doesn't hold a special calling for them, the goal is usually just to survive the physical demands of the rotation.

A surgeon's day starts early, which means that the medical student's day starts even earlier, at approximately 5 or 6 a.m. On a typical day, the student starts by 'rounding' on the floor patients with residents. These patients are either awaiting surgery or have had surgery. Rounding refers to examining the patient and checking surgical wounds, and reviewing vital signs such as blood pressure, heart rate, and respiratory rate. Depending on the circumstances, other data may also be important, such as the amount of urine made over twenty-four hours. The medical student is responsible for checking lab results. A progress note is written in the chart to update the patient's condition at the end of rounds. The rest of the day is spent in the surgical outpatient clinic, operating room, assisting or observing surgeons and residents, and taking care of any other patient issues on the floor, such as ordering medications, filling out discharge forms, drawing blood, inserting intravenous lines and nasogastric tubes. The day ends around five to six p.m. Those who are not on call go home at this point.

Students who are taking call duty with a resident are required to stay till the following day. In some programs, they might be permitted to leave after finishing their work the next morning, but many programs require students to stay until five p.m. the following day, meaning a total of 36 hours on duty. The call schedule varies from once every third to fourth night. Sleep may be possible while on call, but depend entirely on the emergency cases that present in the middle of the night and the condition of the patients on the floor.

In my program, medical students were expected to work directly with patients. Nurses page students on their beepers if they have any concerns about patients, or need any work done. If a resident is beeped by mistake, it doesn't take long before the call is diverted to the student.

A student's participation in the operating room depends on the surgeon. Some will expect students to learn by observing. Others may involve students by allowing them to make small incisions, apply cautery, suture and hold retractors.

Progress Notes

Today was my first day on call in Surgery. Actually, it was my first day on call ever. I had completed the Emergency Rotation two days ago, which had only required twelve hours of shiftwork. Today was the real test.

I yawned my way through the first set of patient rounds with the resident. I wasn't bored, just sleepy after waking up at 5 a.m. to make it to the hospital on time. The second year resident did much of the talking today. I observed and made notes of the questions that seemed most important to him. Surprisingly, they rarely changed from one patient to the next.

How are you, Mr. Bradley? Passed any gas? Moved your bowels yet? As a medical student, I understood the surgical resident's inquiries into the less pleasant aspects of our bodily functions. They are some of the best signs of a body recovering from major surgery. They also determined if the patient's diet would be advanced from fluids to something more substantial. That said, it is still hard to get used to hearing, and even harder for patients to answer without showing embarrassment or discomfort. As one patient responded: "No, I haven't done my business yet. But thanks for asking."

I performed one of the time-honored tasks of the medical student later that day - holding a retractor for the surgeon as he cut out a cancerous growth in a patient's large intestine. This was after I had changed surgical gloves twice for contaminating myself before the surgery began. Gloved hands are only supposed to touch sterile surfaces. The first time was when I reached to adjust my glasses that were getting fogged up by my breath under the surgical mask. (The trick is to pinch the surgical mask tightly at the bridge of the nose so the heated exhaled air doesn't travel upwards). The second time was when I was asked by a nurse to pull the overhead lights over the patient's body. Eager to please, I had reached up with my newly gloved hand, and touched the unsterilized handle of the lights. I failed to see the plastic handle that would have prevented contamination had I used it. Off came the second pair of gloves.

By the time the surgeon entered the room, I had received strict admonishments from the surgical nurses about what I could and could not do. My main duty was to stand with folded arms at the far edge of the patient's body. And I wasn't to move.

I felt like a smurf. Dressed in blue from head to toe, I wore a sky-blue billowy cap over my hair. A blue surgical mask covered my nose and mouth. A thin paper gown lay over my scrubs, and blue booties covered my shoes.

The surgeon put me to task immediately. To compensate for my height, a step stool was provided. Over the next four hours, I held the retractor exactly as the surgeon wanted, and tried to answer all his questions on the patient's anatomy as he removed a gallbladder. "What muscle is this? What blood vessel travels here?" The first question was easy. As for the blood vessel, I was momentarily thrown off as it appeared white. I was used to the brown color of a cadaver. I made a mental note to be better prepared for the next surgery.

I attended the outpatient clinic of another surgeon during the afternoon. Some patients were returning for follow-up visits from their surgery, and some were being seen for the first time to be assessed for possible surgery. My idea of the typical surgical patient was completely changed today. Instead of a geriatric population, many patients were below their fifties. One patient was only twenty. She was accompanied by her father. She had been referred by her Family Physician after her potassium level on a recent blood test was found to be suspiciously low. In addition, her blood pressure was higher than expected. She stated that she had been feeling tired for a number of months. These signs pointed to Conn's syndrome, a disease due to overactive adrenal glands. The glands sit on top of both kidneys and produce chemicals necessary for survival. In her case, it was producing an excess of a hormone called aldosterone. The computerized tomography (CT) scan confirmed a small growth on the left gland. The surgeon explained that the tumour was likely benign. This meant that it didn't have the ability to spread like a malignant cancer. She would, however, need surgery to remove it. He explained the procedure in intricate surgical detail, and father and daughter nodded their heads throughout his explanation. The patient duly signed the informed consent documents before she left.

The experience left me unsettled. If I hadn't understood everything that the surgeon had spoken about, how could two laymen? The surgeon had kept emphasizing that the surgery would be done laprascopically. But what did that mean? He explained where the trocars would be placed. What were trocars? I don't know how much information the patient took away with her, but I would receive my education about laprascopy and trocars later that day.

I was on call with the senior resident for the night. He paged me around 12:30 a.m. and asked me to meet him in the Emergency Room. The E.R. was just as busy as I had left it two nights ago. But this time, I walked in with my head a little higher. I was there as part of the Surgical Consult Team now. The resident said that he wanted me to take down the histories and do physical exams on two patients. He had already met with them, and they were relatively stable for now. After that, I could tell him my diagnosis and management plan. He had called the Surgeon at home, and we would be going to the Operating Room as soon as he arrived. Handing me two consult forms, he left to find a bed in a call room.

After my E.R. rotation, doing a history and physical exam wasn't a scary prospect. I approached my first patient and introduced myself as a medical student from the Department of Surgery. He shook my hand, wincing in pain. Mr. Albert was a 40 year old lawyer, and his abdomen had been hurting since after lunch. He was also nauseated, and now reluctant to move from his bed because the pain on his lower right side was getting worse.

I felt like a detective at that point - trying to find clues to the diagnosis. Mr. Albert had no other symptoms. He was otherwise healthy, except for a smoking habit. During my physical exam, I searched for a surgical scar that would indicate a previous appendectomy, but didn't find one. I felt confident that the patient was showing the classic signs of appendicitis, just as is described in textbooks. I moved his right leg in different directions, looking for the psoas and obturator sign to confirm my diagnosis. I quickly finished my notes as the patient was rolled away to the Radiology Department for films.

My next patient was Mrs. Grisham, a soft-spoken, 58 year old mother of four daughters. She complained of a bloated abdomen. She said she had experienced bloating on and off over the past year. She had lost fifteen pounds in the same amount of time, without dieting. She had no other symptoms. Her family doctor had ordered a number of tests, but nothing had shown up. She decided to come to the E.R. because it was causing her pain for the first time today.

On examination, her abdomen was rounded and taut. She had mild pain when I pressed on it. The resident had decided to admit her for further workup. In Mrs. Grisham's case, I suspected an obstruction of her large bowel, similar to a case I had seen in the Emergency Room last month. The weight loss was also a concern, and I noted it down. Cancer is notorious for causing unexplained weight loss.

As I later reviewed the Xrays taken in the E.R., the pattern of a bowel obstruction could be seen. The loops of the intestine were dilated from air, and fluid was settled on the lower edges. The resident had already scheduled Mrs. Grisham for a CT scan in the next hour.

I spent the early hours of the morning as the surgeon's first assistant as we removed Mr. Albert's inflamed appendix. Medical students are rarely the only assistant in the Operating Room, but the senior resident had been called to deal with a critical patient in the Intensive Care Unit. That left only me. The surgeon decided to remove the appendix laprascopically. This meant making small incisions on the patient's abdomen, and inserting a fiber-optics camera to visualize the appendix. Then, pointed metal rods, or trocars, are inserted. Guided by the video images, the appendix was removed.

It takes two people to perform a laprascopic procedure such as this one. The surgeon patiently guided my first awkward movements as I attempted to control the camera for him. Through the tiny camera, the patient's internal tissues appeared smooth, and they glistened under the camera's light. Over the next hour, the patient's swollen appendix was removed successfully. The surgeon allowed me to 'close' or sew up the small incisions that he had made on the patient's abdomen, watching carefully as I attempted to create neat stitches. As I left the Operating Room, I remember putting my hand on my chest to see if I could feel my pounding heart. As tired as I was, it had also been an exhilarating experience and one that is unusual for a student.

The excitement of the night quickly gave way to just trying to keep my eyes open the next day. My shift didn't end until 5 p.m. that day, when I finally managed to drag myself home and drop my body on the mattress.

Follow-up:

Mr. Albert recuperated in the hospital for three days before being discharged home. Mrs. Grisham was taken to surgery, and was found to have a large tumor on the right colon. (Interestingly, as doctors get better at finding left-sided tumors through colonoscopy, tumors seem to be shifting to the right side where they are harder to detect). The tumor was removed, but because there was evidence of cancer beyond the intestines, she was referred to an Oncologist for consideration for chemotherapy or radiation therapy.

Despite the tragic news, her pleasant demeanor never changed. I visited her daily after my work ended, meeting her husband and daughters on many occasions. "I have been blessed with a good life," she told me, as she sat surrounded by them. That same gentleness that I had seen in her in the Emergency Room was present in her entire family. I lost count of how many time tears threatened to overwhelm me in their presence.

Many patients' faces eventually become a blurred memory, but Mrs. Grisham will always stand out vividly for me. More than being my first personal experience of a patient with cancer, she led me to realize that there are people who have the fortitude to withstand the worst possible reality, and don't let their illness define them. I suspect that she was of much more comfort to me than I was to her at that point in my training.

Internal Medicine

Internal medicine was the most dreaded rotation for most of us in third year of medical school. The senior medical students had warned us beforehand: eat, sleep and urinate when you can, because you may not get another chance. Like

Surgery, Internal Medicine is an extremely busy rotation, and patients tend to be very sick. Students will deal with patients in crisis at least a few times a day.

Doctors who practice Internal Medicine are called Internists. Some practice General Internal Medicine, where they diagnose and treat non-surgical problems of an adult's organ systems, both in the hospital and clinic settings. There are many categories of sub-specialists who have trained in Internal Medicine as well as a second narrowly defined field, such as Cardiology, Gastroenterology, Infectious Diseases and Hematology.

A firm understanding of Internal Medicine and its principles is necessary for all doctors, regardless of specialty. The medical student's learning curve during the two to three months spent in this rotation is steeper than all the others because of the volume of information. In no other rotation is the student's small white medical coat loaded down with books, tendon hammer, ophthalmoscope, tuning fork, and EKG interpretation guides more than in Internal Medicine. In addition to the intellectual challenge, the call schedule requires students to spend every third night in the hospital, usually without sleep for over 24 hours.

There are numerous opportunities to hone your practical skills during the rotation. These include practicing effective ways of obtaining the patient's history, learning specific diagnostic skills such as listening for 'crackles' in the patient's lungs, doing blood-draws and inserting intravenous lines, interpreting urine and blood tests, and participating in procedures like paracentesis (withdrawing fluid from the patient's abdomen).

Students will be assigned a few patients on the hospital floor, and it will be their responsibility, under the supervision of a resident, to check on the patient's daily progress. Each morning begins with rounds with the Attending Physician, residents and nursing staff. The student is required to present a brief history of the patient and reason for hospitalization, scheduled tests, plans for treatment and bring up any issues that need to be addressed. These issues may include discussing the need for physical therapy and rehabilitation following discharge, or arranging for a social worker to meet with the patient.

Following morning rounds, the remainder of the day is spent admitting new patients, following up on lab and diagnostic tests, checking and ordering new medications, attending outpatient clinics and teaching sessions by Attendings and residents. Students may be expected to pick an interesting case to present to the medical staff at the end of the rotation.

From the beginning, the student will be expected to function as part of the team. Hospital staff relies on each other to ensure that the patient's needs are met, and students and residents play a key role in the patient's care. As the resident becomes more comfortable with the student's level of knowledge and sense of responsibility, he or she will start to depend more on the student's account of events at the end of the day rather than check up on all the individual details related to the patient's care.

Progress Notes

The beeper that I kept positioned next to my shoulder emitted a loud signal at around three in the morning. I groaned as I reached out to silence it, my eyes still heavily laden with sleep. The return beeper number on the pager belonged to the senior resident. I was in the second week of my internal medicine rotation, and had averaged an hour of sleep on each call night so far. It looked like my rest was over for tonight.

Each call room in the hospital contains the basic essentials - an uncomfortable bed, sheets, pillow and a telephone. I phoned Warren at the number he had left on the pager. As usual, Warren had an upbeat friendly tone, even this early in the morning. He described a patient in the Emergency Room that needed to be admitted onto our service, and asked me to take the admission. I was still struggling to find the part of me that was happy to be woken up, and assured myself that, in time, I would get used to it. I told him I would be right down.

Mr. Hopnik was my third admission for the night. I found him on a stretcher in the Emergency Room, and immediately developed a liking for the 68 year old retired teacher. He said he had come to the hospital because of difficulty breathing that night. He described episodes of feeling lightheaded at home over the past few weeks, particularly when urinating. He had a rare blood disorder that was being worked up by his doctor, but no other problems. As a relative newcomer to the hospital, I still hadn't learnt the skill of doing a focused physical exam, so I always erred on the side of caution and did a full physical exam on my patients, afraid that I would miss some important clinical finding if I neglected a thorough exam of every organ system.

To my surprise, I didn't hear much of anything in Mr. Hopnik's lungs. But I did find an enlarged liver and spleen. After discussion with the resident, we ordered a panel of tests for his blood, heart, lungs and liver. Shortly after I finished his admissions note, I was paged to the floor to attend to another patient.

The next three hours passed by quickly. Before I knew it, I had to start preparing for morning rounds. I had six patients that I would need to present to the Attending

Physician. I dropped by each patient's bedside, scanned their morning vital signs, examined them, and then returned to the computer to jot down their latest lab results. When I got to Mr. Hopnik's screen, what I saw made me gasp. His liver function tests indicated that his liver was failing. I moved Mr. Hopnik's case to the top of my list, intending to discuss him first on my list of patients with the Attending.

My watch indicated that I was running a few minutes late for morning rounds, so I gathered my notes and rushed to the E.R.. The Attending had already started seeing patients admitted by the intern and residents. We spent over an hour in the Emergency Room, seeing a stroke patient and an elderly female with an esophageal motility disorder. There was one case of an elderly diabetic male admitted with a fever, and the workup had yet to find a source of the infection in him. As the Attending listened to his lungs, he indicated an area on the front of the patient's chest and asked the medical students to listen with our stethoscopes. I heard faint crackles, which I wouldn't have picked up had it not been specifically pointed out. The Attending diagnosed the patient with pneumonia, although the x-ray hadn't shown any definitive signs of one. (A repeat x-ray the following day showed the beginnings of a lobar pneumonia).

It was now almost 8 a.m., and time for morning report. Every morning, the entire Internal Medicine staff of the hospital met in a conference room to discuss interesting or complex cases admitted overnight. Our team agreed to risk being slightly late so we could round on Mr. Hopnik.

His two sons were by the bedside when we entered as an entourage. Mr. Hopnik appeared comfortable, and denied any symptoms of abdominal pain, nausea, shortness of breath or any of the other symptoms that the senior resident rapidly fired at him. We discussed the patient's high liver function tests with him, and Mr. Hopnik stated that his own doctor had mentioned something about an enlarged liver to him previously. The Attending asked me to obtain Mr. Hopnik's old records after morning rounds to get a better handle on his condition. Mr. Hopnik appeared comfortable for now. His first few tests had eliminated the possibility of a pulmonary embolism and heart attack. The Attending and Senior Resident speculated whether a recent antibiotic that he had been prescribed by his Family Doctor was causing the dramatic rise in the liver function tests, as the patient reported taking double the prescribed dose over the past week.

A nurse paged me twenty minutes after I had left the floor to let me know that she had put Mr. Hopnik on 4 liters of oxygen by nasal cannula as he was having some difficulty breathing. I left the conference room and rushed to his bedside. His sons told me that their father had just returned from the bathroom when he began complaining of shortness of breath, similar to episodes he had at home. Mr.

Hopnik appeared pale, and was quietly gasping for breath, but was able to talk. I examined his heart and lungs, but couldn't identify anything wrong. I let him know that I was going to call for an urgent x-ray, EKG and increase the oxygen level. Letting the nurse know of my intentions, I immediately paged the senior resident. He called me back, and I was in the midst of explaining the patient's situation when the nurse frantically ran up to me and said that Mr. Hopnik had become unconscious.

Running back into the room, I saw Mr. Hopnik paler than I had left him, and slumped against his pillow. His two sons were holding his hands and repeatedly calling out to him. I searched frantically for a carotid pulse but didn't find one. "We need to call a code 99, now!" I shouted. Naïve to the procedures of this new hospital, I asked the desk clerk to announce the code over the hospital speakers, as was the procedure in other hospitals that I had rotated through. She shook her head and said I would have to push the blue button in the room. "What blue button?" I remember asking myself as I ran back into the room. Seeing a small button marked 'CODE' above the patient's bed, I pressed it, but nothing happened. However, within seconds, a loud voice announced the patient's room number over the hospital intercom system. Mechanically, it repeated: 'Code 99…Code 99'.

In less than a minute, the code response team appeared flying down the hospital corridors. The respiratory therapist and senior resident began intubating the patient, and an Attending from the ICU took charge of the code. Around 15 staff members now surrounded the patient, each listening to the ICU Attending's directions and doing their own part. A nurse escorted the patient's sons into a waiting area. The Attending began issuing orders for a larger intravenous line and medications. The code cart EKG monitor showed electrical activity of the heart, but the rhythm was erratic.

"Who knows the patient?" he asked, looking around the room. The senior resident looked at me and nodded. I hesitated for a brief second, then stepped forward and started recounting the patient's history. My mouth was dry, and I wasn't sure if the words coming out my mouth were making any sense at that moment. The Attending listened to my account, and then asked me to feel for a pulse on Mr. Hopnik's right arm. I lifted his arm and started to check, when a nurse pushed his arm flat on the bed and told me to check it in that position. I realized my mistake immediately. In a patient whose body was struggling to circulate blood, a pulse would not be felt unless it was in a recumbent position. I felt nothing.

After pushing medications intended to stabilize the heart, and using electric paddles, a regular beat was captured. The Attending issued orders for the patient to be wheeled immediately to the ICU.

I was the last person to leave the room. I found myself trembling, mentally and physically exhausted, and praying for Mr. Hopnik's survival.

I later tried to explain the course of events to my Attending Physician, but found myself unable to remember exact details that would have normally rolled off my tongue. I even struggled to remember the patient's name at one point. In retrospect, I realized that it was a combination of frustration and exhaustion. This was the first code that I been directly involved in. I struggled to find answers to what I could have done differently to affect the outcome.

Since my team had been on call overnight, we were allowed to leave the hospital by midday as long as our work was finished. Unable to disengage myself from the floor, I kept trying to find more work to do until I was the last person on the team still to leave. My Attending Physician, who had come up in the middle of the afternoon to see the patients again, approached me at the computer terminal and gently advised me to go home and get some rest.

The one resource that is always at a premium in hospitals is time, especially for busy clinicians. However, on this day, time took a pause as the Attending listened to me. I struggled to make sense of the morning's events. He didn't interrupt, and kept listening until I had no more words left to express my emotions. Then, he spoke to me about how medical students can become crushed by the demanding hours and personal investment in patients that is an inescapable part of becoming a doctor. He didn't offer any quick fixes to the grief that I was experiencing, and I understood that there were none.

Although Mr. Hopnik's care had passed on to the ICU team, our team visited his bedside daily to check his progress. Mr. Hopnik was placed on dialysis the following day when his kidneys failed. Other organ systems shut down over the next few days until he was being sustained solely by machines. He never regained consciousness. The exact cause for Mr. Hopnik's liver failure was never found. All tests for viruses and diseases that may have accounted for the liver failure came back normal. His family made the decision to remove him from life support five days later.

For the first time since I had started working with patients, I experienced a sense of helplessness. Feelings of frustration lingered for months. I couldn't explain the personal sense of loss that I felt during that time. I had been taken aback with the unexpected outcome, and it brought out emotions that had been pent up from dealing with disease and death daily. The kinship with Mr. Hopnik had formed over just a few hours, but his memory endures with me.

Pediatrics

It has been my experience that Pediatricians are some of the most patient and gentle of physicians. Their ability to bond with a toddler, draw out clues about the illness from a non-verbal, crying child, and soothe parents' anxieties simultaneously are some of the hardest tasks to accomplish. Yet, good Pediatricians do so with ease, humor and confidence.

For the medical student, four to eight weeks in the Pediatrics rotation is spent taking care of admitted patients on the hospital floors, in the Pediatric Emergency Department, and in outpatient general and specialty clinics. Taking call is required only when working on the hospital floors. Students can expect to stay overnight in the hospital every fourth night. Medical students receive greater supervision from residents in this rotation than on the adult medical floors. This is welcomed by most, as many don't have the parental experience to know what to do with a crying child, much less a crying, sick child.

There is a significant amount of interaction with parents in this rotation. Adults become more flustered and worried about their children's health than their own, and a significant part of treating children is reassuring and educating parents. Pediatrics is an enjoyable rotation for most students. The hectic and chaotic environment of Internal Medicine and Surgery is missing here. Physicians and residents tend to operate at a reasonable pace when it comes to children, and medical students are therefore able to follow along easily. There are different levels of care within a pediatric setting. At its most heart-wrenching is the Neonatal Intensive Care Unit, where fragile premature babies not much larger than the size of a palm can be found. Next up is the Special Care Nursery, reserved for babies with mild problems such as jaundice, who require less intensive monitoring and care. The general nursery is for healthy newborns, who are observed for forty-eight hours prior to being discharged home.

Older children are admitted to the general floors. Tertiary care pediatric hospitals, which are equipped to provide a higher level of care, will have specialized floors. One floor may be dedicated to cardiac patients, another to those with infectious diseases, and so forth.

Students may get an opportunity to work in outpatient clinics in larger hospitals as well. Here, children are brought for evaluation of growth, developmental concerns, psychiatric issues and eating disorders. At the community level, pediatricians deal with preventative and primary care of infants and children in their offices.

Progress Notes

My month long rotation in Pediatrics had me assigned to the Cardiac floor. It was a floor dedicated to babies and infants who had been born with heart defects. Some had already undergone several surgeries to correct the anomalies, but were admitted to this floor even if they showed up with the stomach flu or a bad cold because of their past history.

My first patient was a 20 month old child, Jay. He was known as a frequent flyer in the hospital, meaning that he had a long history of frequent hospitalizations. This time, a viral chest infection led to his admission. He had been diagnosed with a cardiomyopathy within the first few months of life. This had caused his heart to enlarge and weaken over time, and led to heart failure. Jay would get fatigued with little activity. His mother said his appetite had decreased, and his growth was starting to slow down.

Other than being a little thin, Jay did not appear to be a child suffering from a severe heart condition. His cheeks were always flushed, and although the rosy glow looked deceptively healthy on him, it was a sign of his decreased exercise tolerance. He was a candidate for a heart transplant, but the family didn't know how much longer they would have to wait.

Jay did not seem to have much liking for me or any of the hospital staff, but he delighted in playing with my heavy, black stethoscope. I got in the habit of swabbing my stethoscope clean before entering his room and giving him free rein with it. Listening to his heart and lungs became a game between us. I would first listen to his wheezing lungs with the stethoscope, and he would imitate me. Then, we would listen to his heart. He had a gallop rhythm, where all four heart sounds could be heard. In most children and adults, only two heart sounds are normally heard.

Jay's infection was getting better slowly, but his heart wasn't showing any improvement. In fact, each day led to further deterioration. Jay remained my patient for the entire month. He recovered from the cold, but the heart failure prevented us from discharging him safely. The last line of my progress notes in his chart always ended with 'Awaiting heart transplant'.

Once I had left the rotation, I didn't think that I would see Jay again. But it was a year later, as I was walking down the hospital corridor sipping a cup of coffee, that a healthy-looking child came crashing into me as he rounded a corner. He looked at me with a mischievous grin, pushed me aside with his pudgy hands and kept on running. It took a moment, but I recognized Jay. His mother appeared around the corner in quick chase of her son. Recognition flared in her eyes as she saw me, and she greeted me warmly. Jay had received a heart transplant at the

Hospital for Sick Children about a year ago. He was back at the hospital that day for a routine checkup, and was now a chubby, active three year old. His activity was no longer limited by his heart, and as if to prove this point, he drew his mother into a chase down the yellow hospital corridors once again.

There is much joy and hope when working with children. It is hard not to be affected by their infectious enthusiasm. My next rotation in Psychiatry, however, would prove to be a direct contrast.

Psychiatry

Students without prior familiarity with psychiatric patients will view this rotation as an eye-opener. The biggest revelation for me was that mental illness is often more incapacitating than a physical illness. Depression, manic-depression, schizophrenia - most people have heard of these illnesses. The true extent of their debilitating powers is often underestimated and dismissed. It brings life to a screeching halt for these victims. Their families suffer along with them. Like many physical conditions, these conditions can be managed, but cures are rare.

The four week rotation in Psychiatry is divided among the inpatient ward, outpatient clinics and emergency room call. Students work closely with residents when patients need to be admitted to the Psychiatric Unit from the E.R.. They learn how to take an appropriate history, with special attention to drug and alcohol abuse which worsen any form of mental illness. Some patients will be violent, and security guards will provide a physical barrier when necessary.

Students will be given a chance to practice their interview skills with patients under the supervision of psychiatrists, and take part in group therapy sessions. The most striking feature of this rotation is the luxury of time that is devoted to each patient, allowing the student to gain a good understanding of the patient as a person rather than just a disease process.

Progress Notes

The first part of my Psychiatric rotation had me scheduled as the only medical student in one wing of the Psychiatric ward of the largest hospital in the city. The day started at 8 a.m. instead of the early hours that I had become used to by now. I was discouraged from wearing my white jacket during this rotation. Given the extra time for sleeping, and the opportunity to rid myself of my starched coat, there was an extra spring in my step as I bounded up to the Psychiatric Unit on the first day.

My responsibility was to follow six admitted patients during the month. I would see them every morning and write progress notes in their charts. Once a week, the Psychiatrist and I would meet to discuss their progress and further plans for management.

My afternoons were spent either in Outpatient clinics or working with Psychiatric residents in the Emergency Department and the temporary Psychiatric Hold area. The Hold area was adjacent to the Emergency Room. It contained 3 padded cells that could only be locked from the outside, and 16 single rooms arranged around a large nursing station. These rooms housed short-term admitted patients until they were well enough to be discharged, or until a place was found for them in a long-term facility.

My first patient on the inpatient ward was a young male, admitted against his will for a schizophrenic relapse. He had been 'pinked' or 'certified' in the Emergency Room. This meant that two physicians had signed a legal document stating that the patient was either a danger to himself or society, and needed immediate hospitalization. Such an order could keep a person involuntarily for examination for three days.

Tim had a long history of mental illness. He had started hearing voices in his twenties, and acted on them violently three years ago. His past medical record revealed that he had taken a pair of scissors and stabbed his left eye several times at the behest of the voice. His eye had to be surgically removed, and a prosthetic one was placed. On that same hospitalization, he had tried to jump out his hospital window, and had succeeded in breaking the window by hurling his body against it.

These two episodes marked his first psychotic break. The next year was spent in a long-term facility, where Tim improved considerably. He was able to move back into his parent's home, and although he continued to struggle with the isolation that most schizophrenics face, he did find employment. Recently, though, he had begun to feel that co-workers were talking about him. Unable to tolerate the perceived looks and comments, Tim had stopped going to work, and shut himself inside his bedroom. A week prior to hospitalization, he had started to refuse food and psychiatric medications. He stopped communicating with his family. Fearing another psychotic episode, his parents had brought him in desperation to the Emergency Room.

The idea of interviewing Tim alone in his hospital room made me nervous. According to the Attending Physician's progress notes, Tim hadn't improved much since hospitalization a week ago. He had yet to get out of bed.

Prior to entering his room, I let a nurse know that I would be interviewing Tim. She asked me to keep the door open. I was comforted that his room was right next to the nursing station. I knocked twice on the door. There was no response.

The lights were off, but some light streamed in through the small window on the opposite corner of the room. Usually, rooms of this size housed two patients, but Tim was kept isolated for now.

Tim's lanky figure was sprawled out, face down, on the bed. He didn't turn to look at me as I entered. I introduced myself, and asked permission to speak with him. He didn't say anything initially, and I found my level of discomfort rising each second. Finally, I heard a quiet 'okay'.

Tim only spoke in three or four word sentences the first day. His affect, or the way that he spoke and appeared, was completely flat. Without emotion. He seemed to be separate from his own words. He continued to hear voices, and said that he didn't want to come out of his room as everyone was talking about him. Our first conversation lasted less than five minutes, as he had stopped answering my questions after that point. I thanked him and left. The psychiatrist had started him on a new regimen of psychotropic medications, and we had yet to see if it would make any difference in his mood and behavior.

Tim made slow progress through the month, but by the end of the four weeks, he was ready to come outside his bedroom and take an occasional walk down the hallway. Some days, he appeared more morose than others and would refuse to talk. But there was no denying that a shift had occurred when he greeted me one day in the hallway with a nod. The voices had stopped but he still feared that others were out to persecute him.

Tim spent a few more weeks on the ward after my rotation ended, and eventually returned to his parent's home. He had lost his job. His medications were changed on discharge. Instead of taking daily doses, he now needed to show up once a week at a neighborhood clinic for a shot. This would allow mental health nurses to assess him frequently, and perhaps allow him to be more compliant with his medications.

Tim is hardly alone in his own personal prison. It is estimated that one percent of the population suffers from schizophrenia. Among the young, the disease's presence is first felt in the twenties, usually during the college years. With the help of medications and strong social support, it is possible for up to a third of schizophrenics to improve. Another third remain the same despite treatment measures, and the remainder continue to decline. Suicide is not an uncommon outcome for them. I left the rotation with the awareness that in no other field is compassion more necessary than in Psychiatry.

Elective Rotations

By the time the fourth year rolls around, students will be ready to let out a sigh of relief. The most challenging rotations like Surgery and Internal Medicine will be over. The hospital environment will be a familiar place, and students will have gathered enough knowledge to feel more at ease with their responsibilities.

The final year is structured for the completion of any remaining required rotations, such as Neurology, Geriatrics and Ambulatory Care. It is also the first opportunity for students to pick their own rotations, known as electives. The main goal of the fourth year is to make a decision regarding a specialty for future practice, and plan for residency. Students will meet with a faculty member, such as the Dean of Student Affairs, to discuss their future plans and obtain a Dean's letter in support of their application. By now, students should have started to identify the fields that interest them. Electives are used as a means of confirming that interest by spending more time in the specialty, and for securing letters of recommendation. Electives offer the best opportunity for working in different kinds of hospitals - public, private, and community. Many schools offer the option of national and international electives, so students can combine travel with clinical duties. By working in different hospitals, students can assess the various residency programs available before making their final choice.

Once the core rotations are completed in third year, there are numerous electives that students can take during their fourth year of medical school. Students interested in Internal Medicine may choose electives in subspecialties like Nephrology or Rheumatology. Future surgeons may decide to spend one month in Plastic Surgery and the next month in Vascular Surgery.

Progress Notes

I chose to do two weeks of a Cardiothoracic Surgery elective. The first day involved holding the retractor while the surgeon added blood vessels to the patient's diseased heart arteries. This type of surgery is called a CABG (pronounced cabbage), which stands for coronary artery bypass grafting. Patients who require it are those at imminent risk of a heart attack due to clogged up heart arteries. Surgeons typically remove veins from the leg, or arteries below the chest wall, to attach to the heart arteries. These are sutured above and below the diseased sections of the arteries, providing an alternate path for blood flow.

The second day, I was promoted to holding the patient's beating heart while the surgeon attached the grafts and placed tiny sutures on it. By the end of the week, I was suturing the patient's leg after the saphenous vein had been removed. Occasionally, the radial artery is removed from the forearm to function as a graft, and I would be given the opportunity to suture the patient's arm as well. The Surgeon advised me to take my time with the stitches, as he wanted a good result. Patient's often judged the success of the surgery by the look of the scar, he warned.

At the end of the surgery, when the patient was being 'closed up', I would assist in placing plastic tubes and drains leading out from the chest, for the purpose of removing excess fluid during the recovery phase. I sewed metal wires through the patient's sternum (breast bone) to close the chest cavity, and stapled the skin edges together. Each surgery lasted between four to six hours, and I was given the freedom to go between operating rooms during the day to gain maximum exposure to patients.

Although I had identified my career interests as being outside the surgical realm by now, the Cardiothoracic Surgery elective provided some of the most gratifying moments of medical school. Seeing a beating heart stop in an ice-water bath, and then watching it brought back to life at the end of surgery is about as invasive as doctors can get in trying to restore health. Seeing it on television documentaries that aim to show real life medicine just isn't the same. All your senses become seared with the memory of that moment.

Another memorable experience during the elective period showed me the work of doctors when they aren't trying to restore health . I arranged to witness an autopsy while working in a community hospital. The pathology labs always seem to be located in the basement of hospitals, which invariably have winding dark corridors and doors without names, adding to their mystery. The smell of the formaldehyde led me towards the lab.

The patient was a male who had expired (a euphemistic medical term for died) the previous night at home. The law states that any patient who isn't been under a physician's care at the time of death requires an autopsy. The Pathologist's assistant had prepped the patient by sawing his skull open to expose the brain for an examination. The Pathologist donned a thick apron, and started by forming a Y-shaped cut on the patient's chest and abdomen. I wasn't prepared for the overpowering smell that emanated from the deceased's intestines. I remember looking desperately at the heavy metal doors, wishing that I was on the other side of it. One by one, the Pathologist removed the patient's organs and weighed them on a scale. Out came the liver, heart, and kidneys. He kept a small piece of each in a jar to examine under the microscope later. Samples of the patient's blood had been sent for the toxicology screen to determine if he had any suspicious substances in his system that might have contributed to his death. But the cause of death, according to the Pathologist, seemed straightforward. He had found a large clot in the patient's lungs, and attributed his death to a pulmonary embolism.

International Elective

My next elective provided me with an experience that went beyond the confines of western medicine. How could one say no to a taste of medicine in the Fiji Islands? For one month, I rotated through a tertiary care hospital in the capital city, which served as a referral center for the most complex cases in the country.

The hospital was established at the turn of the century, and was an old, beautiful colonial structure, left over from the days of British imperialism. Most of its doctors were former graduates of the only medical school in the country.

A typical day started by rounding on the patients in the Internal Medicine ward. While patients in the U.S. are termed private versus service patients depending on their level of insurance, the distinction in Fiji was not so subtle. Patients were either in the 'Paying' or 'Non-Paying' Wards. Free medical care is the right of all patients in this developing country, but the ability to pay greatly enhanced the services that were made available. The paying ward contained private rooms, while the non-paying ward was made up of large open floors, with about twenty beds each. Patients could see each other quite openly unless the curtains were used, although I didn't see any curtains drawn the whole month. Privacy wasn't a consideration. Cases were discussed openly, within hearing distance of at least four other patients.

The types of patient problems that I encountered on the wards were not much different from here. Pneumonia, congestive heart failure, heart attacks, strokes - these were abundant. A few things were striking though. Patients were encouraged to have a family member present with them to assist with their feeding and bathing. Patients who needed a blood transfusion first had to find a family or friend willing to donate an equal amount of blood in exchange for the blood they would receive. Many of the cases encountered were so far advanced that patient's diseases were identifiable at first glance, as in the case of a patient with scleroderma, a disease of the connective tissue resulting in skin that appears shiny and taut across the face. As this patient was walking down the corridor towards our clinic, the Attending challenged me to guess the diagnosis based on her appearance. Another similar case was of a patient with acromegaly. This is a disease where abnormal amounts of growth hormone are secreted, resulting in features such as large hands and feet. Patients will typically complain of an increasing shoe and ring size. The disease was easily identifiable in this patient from his distorted facial features. He had thick skin, a protruding jaw and brow, and prominent nose and lips. If treatment is delayed, acromegaly can lead to premature death. In most cases, patients at the hospital presented fairly late for diagnosis and treatment of their illnesses, as many lived in rural areas or outlying islands.

While the term pheochromocytoma may not mean much to you, it is a unique condition, and one that most physicians only read about but never get an opportunity to see. I was able to see an 18 year old male with this disease, and watched as his father refused surgery, proclaiming fear for his son's life during the procedure. As a consequence of the tumor that was causing the disease, the young patient's blood pressure would shoot up to dangerous levels. Without treatment, he was bound to have an early death. The hospital team watched helplessly as the father and son signed papers refusing treatment, and took the next bus back to their village.

Tuberculosis remains a fairly common disease in Fiji, and I was taken aback by the approach taken at the hospital. In the U.S. and Canada, patients who are suspected of harboring the highly contagious disease are immediately isolated from others. Anyone entering the patient's room is required to wear a respiratory mask, gown, gloves, and the room itself operates on a pressure gradient so that air doesn't leak out into the hallway. If Fiji, however, patients who are suspected of having the disease are not isolated until the biopsy taken from the lung provided definitive proof of the disease. At this point, they were transferred to another facility for treatment. The Attending physician, residents, nurses and students did not wear face masks around the suspected cases, and I later found out that these masks weren't even available in the hospital. As one physician explained, they considered the probability of a healthy person contracting the disease as being so low that it didn't justify the cost of additional precautions. The lifetime risk for healthy people exposed to the tubercle bacilli is about ten percent.

While North American hospitals have their own share of tragic cases, the patients that I encountered in the Intensive Care Unit of this facility still haunt me. I came across a female patient who had been strangled by her husband to the point of becoming comatose. She was now intubated in the ICU, and had failed to regain consciousness. I watched her helpless body lying attached to the machines and wondered about the care of her child if she didn't survive. The clear marks of the blue and black bruises from the attacker's fingers lay as evidence on her exposed neck.

While this patient, who was most likely brain-dead from lack of oxygen during the attack, occupied one of the scarce ICU beds, another young comatose patient was admitted overnight to the general ward. She was suspected to have viral encephalitis, an infection which had led to brain swelling. Although her vital signs were stable, she was at clear risk of being unable to breathe on her own if the swelling continued. It is impossible to predict her final outcome had an ICU bed been available for her, but in a place where resources are scarce, it wasn't too surprising when the twenty-seven year old patient died quietly overnight.

In the short time that I spent in the country, I had many opportunities to see tropical illnesses that I had not been taught about in medical school. One case was that of a 26 year old male who had gone scuba diving around the reefs late at night.

Although he was an experienced diver and familiar with safety around sea animals, his inability to visualize an approaching sting ray led to a month's hospitalization. Sting rays are large, rhomboid shaped fish related to the shark family. They have a distinctive long tail with sharp spines containing venom to fight off predators. That particular night, the unsuspecting diver was whipped by the sting ray's tail on his right leg, resulting in multiple ragged lacerations. The pain was immediate and excruciating. He was bleeding heavily, and also complained of nausea, muscle cramps and weakness. His diving partner had brought him by motorboat straight from the reef to the hospital.

At the time of admission, the patient's leg had swollen to more than double its size. As the physician stabilized his low blood pressure and bleeding, he explained that such bites can be lethal if the sting ray punctures the lungs or abdomen. As the days passed, the pain subsided and swelling decreased. Using an old walker for physical therapy, the patient worked relentlessly on his ambulation until he was well enough to be discharged. Last I heard, he still goes diving in the middle of the night.

Since I had arranged the international elective to take place just prior to my vacation, I had the chance to explore the country's outlying islands after the elective ended. My travels on an open air bus along dusty roads led to many opportunities to discuss medicine, both western and traditional, with the local islanders. At one point, I found myself discussing high blood pressure and its treatment with a local bus rider on a long journey. At a rest stop, I was asked by a number of the Fijian men and women to take their blood pressure measurements. Although access to regular medical care was a problem for many, I got a chance to speak to them about exercise, weight loss and diet at the bus-stop. In return, they showed me a cactus-like plant growing by the roadside, used in traditional Fijian medicine for treating wounds and skin irritations. I later found out that the cactus-like plant had been aloe vera.

In another instance, I was humbled when I was approached by a woman in a rural part of the country for advice on her son who had been diagnosed with cancer. Hearing that I was from 'overseas', synonymous with excellent medical care, she brought along his medical reports with her. While my knowledge on his form of leukemia was limited, I was grateful for the medical text that I had packed into my bag at the last minute. At the very least, I was able to talk to her about the disease process and its treatments.

The journey back to North America also became memorable. On the trans-Pacific flight from Fiji to Los Angeles, a passenger developed sudden breathing difficulty. The Flight Attendant asked for any doctor on board to identify himself, as immediate assistance was needed. A minute went by, and surprisingly, there didn't appear to be any MD's on that flight. I waved over an Attendant and asked if I, as a medical student, could be of help. He led me to the patient's seat, and it quickly became apparent that she was likely having an allergic reaction to the seafood served for dinner. She had also developed large red welts over her face and arms. With some oxygen, reassurance and an anti-histamine from the airplane's first-aid kit, the patient started to feel better. I am not sure what I would have done had it been something beyond my understanding. I am glad I didn't have to find out.

I returned from my trip with a renewed enthusiasm for medicine. The medical school model in North America often makes students redundant in the hospital during their clinical years, and we don't realize that we have become capable of providing meaningful care. The parts of the world where need is greatest offers some of the best opportunities for using your skills and learning new ones. Students returning from remote parts of Africa had played important roles, such as first assist, in major surgeries. Any student interested in an international health elective should try to gain such unique experiences. This is a valuable time for learning, and remember, you are still paying tuition for the opportunity. Go to an area of the world that is more than just a travel opportunity. The spirit of the people that you encounter will live with you forever. You may find yourself promising to go back again.

As the rotations and electives wind down to a close, you will be closer to graduation day. This also means that it is time to start thinking about the second of the United States Medical Licensing Exams.

USMLE STEP 2 Clinical Knowledge and Clinical Skills

The USMLE Step 2 tests the candidate's ability to practice medicine in a supervised setting. At this point in their education, medical students are being entrusted with additional responsibilities for patient care, and are expected to perform competently and safely. Step 2 provides the licensing authorities an objective means of measuring the students' understanding of normal conditions and disorders, and of the relevant principles in diagnosis and management. Medical ethics, clinical epidemiology and preventive medicine are also assessed.

The Step 2 is conducted over two days. One part tests clinical knowledge through a multiple choice exam, and the other part assesses student's clinical skills through a practical exam. Students registered in an American or Canadian medical school can take Step 1, Step 2 Clinical Knowledge and Step 2 Clinical Skills in any order.

Step 2 Clinical Skills presents the medical student with 11 to 12 standardized patients for 15 minutes each. The student's task is to obtain a thorough history, perform a focused physical exam, document the findings, arrive at a tentative diagnosis and suggest diagnostic studies for work-up. The student is also evaluated on English communication and interpersonal skills during the encounter. The exam is marked as a pass or fail.

The practical portion of the Step 2 is offered at five locations across the United States: Philadelphia, Atlanta, Los Angeles, Chicago and Houston. In addition to the $975 examination fee, students are responsible for their transportation and accommodation expenses.

Final Thoughts:

The last two years of medical school feel less like school and more like full-time work, except that you aren't getting paid yet. Being a part of so many patients' lives leaves you feeling rewarded all the same. Be prepared to be overwhelmed and stressed. There will be many bumps as you slowly transform from someone who knows a lot, to someone who can do a lot. Most importantly, rest up during the summer after graduation. Internship is about to start.

Chapter 13: What Comes after Medical School?

Success is not the key to happiness. Happiness is the key to success. If you love what you are doing, you will be successful.
- Dr. Albert Schweitzer

The post-graduate years (PGY) mark the phase of training after medical school, and is called residency. Though you carry the title of physician at the end of four years of study, there is little that you will be qualified to do on your own. State medical boards will grant licensure to practice clinical medicine independently only after a period of supervised clinical work in hospitals as a resident. This is the time when graduates acquire skills that put their knowledge into practice.

The first year after medical school used to be known as the internship year, and is a term still in common use in teaching hospitals. However, medical schools and the American Medical Association now refer to is as the PGY-1 year. Medical students will start preparing for this year long before graduation rolls around.

Applying for residency entails entering another application process, similar to applying for medical school. The application process starts approximately nine months prior to graduation. In the first half of their fourth year, students submit applications to the Electronic Residency Application Service (ERAS) and the National Resident Matching Program (NRMP). ERAS coordinates the application form, reference letters, transcripts, USMLE scores and Dean's Letter and makes it available to Residency Program Directors. The objective of the NRMP is to match medical school graduates with residency programs for post-graduate training. There are a few notable exceptions. Ophthalmology, Otolaryngology, Plastic

Surgery, Neurological Surgery and Neurology programs don't participate in the NRMP. They have their own residency application process, made available through the San Francisco Match (www.sfmatch.org). Applicants seeking a post-graduate position in Urology have to apply through the American Urological Association Office of Education (www.auanet.org).

After applications are submitted, Program Directors invite candidates for interviews at their hospital. Medical schools allow sufficient free time from clinical duties so that students can travel all over the country attending interviews.

If the Program Director is interested in a particular student joining his program, that student will be ranked highly in the Match. Students find out the results on the third Thursday in March of each year, prior to graduation. Those who don't match to a program of their choice then have the option of applying to all the unfilled programs or waiting until the following year to apply again.

A resourceful online guide on graduate specialty and subspecialty training programs is the Fellowship and Residency Electronic Interactive Database (FREI-DA). It is the electronic version of the Green Book, which can be found in libraries. It allows students to search for information on post-graduate programs throughout the U.S. Access it online at http://www.ama-assn.org/go/freida.

Residency Interviews

General consensus is that residency interviews are far less stressful than those for medical school. Most hospitals will try to convince you to rank their program highly, and will try to make the interview process as pleasant as possible. However, some programs do have a version of the stress interview. In these cases, candidates will be given medically relevant scenarios, and asked how they would handle the situation. For example, how should a patient who comes to the Emergency Room with chest pain be treated? Some hospitals also give a short written test on the interview day.

The morning usually starts with an orientation to the hospital residency program, followed by a tour with a resident. Interviews are conducted one on one either with the Residency Program Director or his designee, or with two or more members of the Residency Committee.

Common Residency Interview Questions
- Why have you chosen this field?
- Why have you applied to this hospital?
- Why should the Program Director choose you over other candidates?
- Where do you see yourself ten years from now?

- What did you enjoy most about medical school?
- What are your weaknesses?
- Do you have any questions about the program?

Program Directors are interested in recruiting the best candidates, and a lot of time is spent emphasizing the unique characteristics of the hospital. Candidates should use the opportunity to get all their questions answered about the program. To get an idea of the quality of the education they will be receiving in the program, inquire about the Board Exam pass rates, opportunities for fellowships, research opportunities and devoted resident teaching hours. Since a minimum of three years will be spent at that particular location, find out about transportation and affordable living arrangements. Some hospitals provide subsidized housing for residents.

Preliminary versus Categorical Programs

Specialty programs require a year of rotating electives during the first year. This 12 month period is known as the preliminary year. Some programs offer the preliminary year at the same location as the hospital where the residency will take place. Others require students to enter the Match to find a separate hospital that will accept them for the year long training period. Internal Medicine, Surgery and Transitional Year Programs offer positions for preliminary training. Some university residency programs have affiliations with community hospitals to provide the preliminary training year for its residents. In these situations, a spot will be reserved at the community hospital for completing the internship. Categorical programs are those which accept students for the entire period of residency. .

In Canada, the process is different. Residency training programs are under the jurisdiction of university programs, not individual hospitals. Distinctions between preliminary and categorical programs are not made. Once students are matched to a residency position, the entire training takes place within that program.

Residency Work Hours

Until recently, there weren't any laws protecting resident's rights when it came to work hours. Working more than a hundred hours a week was commonplace. Years ago, doctors were even required to live on hospital grounds in order to be available at a moment's notice, leading to the term 'resident'. Some states such as New York have compelled hospitals to follow an eighty hour work week rule for a number of years. In 2003, all states across the U.S. adopted the same policy. The 80 hour workweek stipulates that a resident should not work more than this amount, or the hospital will be subject to a fine. It also specifies that residents will be responsible for patients for a maximum of 24 hours at a time, with an additional six hours allowed for sign-over between teams. In addition, they will receive a minimum of ten hours of rest between shifts, and one twenty-four hour period off per week.

Residents are required to be on call in the hospital every third to fourth night. PGY-1 residents take the most number of calls, and with each year of seniority, the call schedule becomes lighter. Most residents start their work around 7 a.m. Surgical programs tend to start earlier, as all admitted patients need to be assessed before going to the Operating Room. A usual workday ends around 5 to 6 p.m.

Residency programs such as Internal Medicine have a night float system in place in some states. This means that residents take 'short' call from Sunday to Thursday, and 'long' call on Friday and Saturday. Short call means working regular daytime hours, and then being on call from approximately 5 p.m. till 11 p.m. At that time, the night float resident receives sign-out about the patients, and assumes care for the patients. The short-call resident resumes regular work hours the following morning at 7 a.m. Long call usually means staying in the hospital for a minimum of twenty-four hours.

Programs that don't offer night float systems require residents to work their regular day hours, and then take on-call responsibility from 5 p.m. till the next morning. At this time, they sign out any active patient issues to the morning team, see their assigned patients, write progress notes, and go home to rest. They return the following morning at 7 a.m.

The hours are long. They may even be the worst part of medical training. The theory is that long hours allow residents to see a patient through the crucial early hours of an illness and minimize the oversight that can occur when transferring care. But it is increasingly being acknowledged that sleep deprivation is a risk for both patients and physicians. Would you feel safe undergoing surgery knowing that the resident has been without sleep for twenty-eight hours? And that he owes his alertness to the fine coffee beans of Peru? Even the most meticulous residents admit that their technical skills and ability to assess patients decline as they become fatigued. Even worse, compassion and empathy become in short supply when residents are physically and mentally drained. The potential harm to patients is obvious, but there are similar risks for residents. In an informal survey of residents during my internship year, the majority reported being so sleep-deprived that they had fallen asleep at stop lights while driving home.

While the PGY-1 year for most programs follows the above schedule, the work hours decrease dramatically for certain residencies from the PGY-2 year onwards. Examples include Dermatology, Ophthalmology, Occupational Medicine and Physical Medicine and Rehabilitation. Since emergencies are unusual in these fields, programs often allow residents to take call from home instead of staying in the hospital overnight.

The first year of residency is one of the most demanding times of a doctor's life. The responsibilities of looking after very sick patients without direct supervision is a terrifying thought initially. Will you know enough to diagnose correctly? Order the right medications? Answer all the patient's and nurses' questions?

The short answer is no. Though the knowledge acquired in medical school feels like it is enough to fill a library, the learning that remains to be done is still tremendous. Every patient becomes your teacher at this stage. Memorized facts suddenly begin acquiring real faces. Patients rarely present with all the classic symptoms found in textbooks, and this is one of the biggest challenges of real medicine. Internship gives the first chance to learn how to weed out the salient points in a patient's history to arrive at the correct diagnosis. For the first time, you will have an opportunity to try to ascertain the patient's condition on your own, without influence from other residents or Attending Physicians. It is only after you have assessed the patient that senior physicians will check your management and offer input.

While the Attending Physician will oversee the care of the patient, the intern orders the medications and tests, writes progress notes, examines the patient daily, draws blood and communicates with family members. They assist residents in admitting patients from the Emergency Room, and then assume care of these patients on the floor.

During the internship year, students rotate through different Departments in the hospital. A typical intern in an Internal Medicine Program would have a schedule of one month in the Emergency Department, one month of electives, one month in an outpatient clinic, one month of holidays, one to two months in an Intensive or Cardiac Care Unit, and the remaining time on the hospital 'floors'.

When patients are admitted to a hospital, they end up on one of several floors. Smaller hospitals might have one floor intended for all medical patients and another dedicated to surgical patients. A large hospital will have several floors for Internal Medicine patients, and each floor will be divided up by specialty. For example, one floor will be for patients with neurological illnesses, another for cancer patients, a third for cardiac patients and so forth.

Interns are often referred to as 'scut monkeys'. This alludes to the enormous amount of mindless work that interns carry out on a daily basis, such as drawing blood and transporting patients to the Radiology Department for tests. The amount of learning that takes place with these tasks is minimal, but they occupy a large chunk of time on a daily basis. The internship year is, without any doubt, a challenge physically and emotionally. It requires a work commitment of at least 80 hours a week, with overnight call every third to fourth night. Surgical programs usually require more. The constant fatigue leaves little time for reading, except during the less intense rotations such as the outpatient clinics and electives.

USMLE Step 3

The third Board Exam, the United States Medical Licensing Exam Step 3, is usually written at the end of the internship year, but may be written up until the end of residency. Medical school graduates who have passed Step 1 and Step 2 are eligible to take the exam. It is computer-based, and is administered over two days. It assesses a physician's clinical judgment and the ability to practice general medicine independently. The exam contains vignettes with multiple choice questions, and a half-day session consisting of clinical encounters using an interactive computer program. Students are asked to assess patient complaints and make clinical decisions in these case scenarios. For further information, visit: www.usmle.org.

Making the transition from medical student to intern is riddled with anxiety, as the focus is now on performance rather than learning. Attending physicians have greater expectations, and challenge interns routinely with questions. The fresh graduates are expected to act as competent physicians, but lack the experience that gives them the confidence to do so. Ultimately, the internship year is about developing the skills and self-assurance that sets a confident resident apart from the inexperienced beginner. Though no one tells you this on your graduation day, it will take months before you are comfortable being addressed as doctor, and a few more after that until you begin to feel worthy of the title. The following account of a day on call during my internship came at a point when I had just started to feel at ease with my role. But did I trust myself with the sickest of patients in the ICU?

A Day in the Life of an Intern: On Call in the ICU

My internship in Internal Medicine took place in a busy New York City hospital. The program was one of the largest in the city, with over eighty interns and residents.

Today, I was covering the Intensive Care Unit. The Chief Resident had paged me on a Friday to tell me that he was assigning me to the ICU the next day as the assigned intern couldn't make it in to work. The next morning, I showed up at 6 am to pre-round on the patients. I wanted to familiarize myself with their conditions before official rounds with the ICU Attending Physician at 8 am.

My only experience with the Intensive Care Unit had been through hearsay from my fourth year colleagues during medical school. The few brave who had chosen it as an elective had described it as confusing. Sophisticated machines and the complex cases of multi-organ failure in the Unit were beyond the grasp of most students. Added to this was that the patients were on a smorgasbord of medications, many of which I had little experience with. Medical students do little more than observe residents and Attendings when they take Intensive Care as an elective, but I didn't have even that experience to fall back on.

I found the overnight intern slumped at the nursing station that morning. He told me that he had just experienced one of the worst nights of his life. One patient went into cardiac arrest seven times. After being shocked back with electric paddles each time, his body had eventually given up at four in the morning. In addition, there were two other critical patients in the Unit, who had required numerous interventions all night. They had made it till morning, and he informed me that they were now my responsibility.

He left me with a list of tasks to accomplish for the day. Normally, he would have checked the bloodwork drawn at 4:30 in the morning and fixed any problems, but he excused himself by saying that the night had been a disaster, and he was leaving it to me. In addition, I would have to assess each of the 16 critically ill patients and write a progress note on them. Plus, could I please start Mr. Avery on an antibiotic since he was spiking a temperature? He had a known heart valve problem, and may have developed endocarditis, an infection in his heart. Could I call his Cardiologist as well? And Mrs. Johnson needed to have blood drawn immediately as she was on a blood thinner. Apparently, the lab assistant hadn't been able to draw her blood at the morning lab rounds.

Overwhelmed already, I attempted to prioritize my tasks, but the day took a life of its own very quickly. One patient expired within the first hour. His had been an expected death, as his breathing tube had been removed during the night at the family's request. The patient had suffered a hemorrhagic stroke, where he had bled in his brain. The Neurologist had determined that the patient's brain activity had ceased. His life was being maintained by machines only at this point, and his family had requested a 'terminal wean'. This phrase referred to detaching the machines from the patient's body, and allowing the patient to pass away. Never having witnessed a terminal wean before, I found myself a little unnerved by the situation. However, there was no time to reflect on it, as the nurse-in-charge approached me to say that the patient's family was in the conference room, and could I speak with them?

Not knowing anything about the patient except his final diagnosis, I quickly familiarized myself with his chart, and met with the family. Amidst their tears and grief, they thanked me for my care. I left the meeting feeling like an imposter. Surely, there was somebody more familiar with the patient who should have met with the family at this time? I called the patient's Attending Physician, and advised him of the patient's death. He commented that he had been just about to start to the hospital, but wouldn't need to come in now.

The desk clerk told me that the Medical Records Department would be calling for the death package soon, and I should have it filled out by then. Not knowing what a death package could possibly be, I asked for clarification. It was the death certificate. My name would be entered on the patient's death certificate as the doctor who had verified and announced the time of death. I hadn't met the patient when he was alive, but my name would be permanently recorded on his resting papers.

As I struggled to catch up with the morning's work, five new patients were admitted to the Intensive Care Unit. As soon as they were stabilized in the Emergency Room by the senior resident, they were brought up to the Unit. The resident paged me to discuss the patients' diagnoses and plans of treatment, and transferred their care to me. Seeing similar diagnoses for each of the patients, it was becoming clear to me that cases repeated themselves in the ICU. There were a handful of previously admitted patients intubated for exacerbation of chronic obstructive pulmonary disease. Almost all were still smoking or had smoked for the greater part of their lives. Another big group were those admitted with chest pain. The majority was likely to test positive for a heart attack over the next twenty-four hours, and would need to be started on a regimen of intravenous and oral cardiac medications. It was my responsibility to keep checking their electrocardiograms to see if they needed to go for immediate angioplasty, where a balloon is used to open up a blocked artery of the heart.

Morning became night, and by 10 p.m., I realized that I had forgotten about dinner. The cafeteria had closed three hours ago. As I munched on vending machine candy bars, I suddenly realized that my beeper had gone a full ten minutes without a page. No time to waste. I busied myself with checking lab results and going over patient charts to catch up with my work.

Suddenly, a loud noise on the cardiac monitor pierced the air. A quick glance at the screen showed a flat line on Mrs. Marion's monitor. Her bed was located less than five feet from where I was standing, and I was the first to arrive at the bedside. The elderly lady, brought in for sudden collapse at her home, was slumped over in her bed. 'ABC's', I reminded myself. The mnemonic for the first action in any emergency was to check airway, breathing and circulation. I checked all three, then started cardiac compressions. By now, I was surrounded by a team of nurses and the crash cart, which held the electric paddles. I prayed that I wouldn't have to use them. With only five compressions, Mrs. Marion regained consciousness, and looked up at us with startled eyes. I was just as surprised as she was, as this was the first time that I had seen a successful code. If a patient has a cardiac arrest in the hospital, the likelihood that he will be discharged at some point is less than twenty percent. By this time, a number of senior doctors had reached the bedside. The Cardiologist and I reviewed Mrs. Marion's heart tracing taken just prior to the event, and found that her electrical rhythm had changed spontaneously, making it impossible for her heart to continue pumping blood. She needed a pacemaker emergently. The cardiologist notified the Cardiac Lab that he was bringing a patient up, and I drew blood and obtained consent for the procedure from Mrs. Marion.

The early hours of the morning saw the admissions of another two patients: one of a young HIV positive male with pneumonia in both lungs, and another of an elderly gentleman with renal failure from multiple myeloma. As morning approached, I scrambled to make notes on all the newly admitted patients. The clerk informed me that Dr. Charest, one of the ICU Directors, would be making rounds that morning. My heart sank. This Attending Physician was unlike any I had ever encountered before. An aristocratic European, he clearly delighted in humiliating residents. His favorite target, unfortunately, was new interns.

We met for rounds at 8 a.m. Two second year residents and three of my fellow interns were also present. Dr. Charest strolled into the ICU and directed his first question at Jon, an intern.

"Did you get dressed in the dark this morning, Jon?"

Jon hesitated, then replied that he hadn't.

"Well, obviously you did, since you aren't wearing a tie. Chris, give him your tie," he ordered, addressing one of the second year residents.

The morning hadn't started well for Jon, and I sensed that all the interns would soon be equally criticized. It wasn't long in coming. Dr. Charest stuck a chest xray on the viewbox, and nodded at me. "Since you look the most disheveled, I take it you were on call overnight. You must know this patient. Read his film."

I stepped forward and centered myself in front of the Xray viewbox. The film belonged to the gentleman with renal failure. I began my interpretation of the black and white chest film, and was quickly cut short.

"No, no, no. Why doesn't any intern ever get it right? You should have an approach," he said, stressing the last word. "Don't tell me the diagnosis. Tell me about the film first."

My heart was pounding in my throat. The lack of sleep was making me dizzy. I attempted to do as he asked, but was cut off again.

"Looks like you didn't pay much attention in Radiology in medical school. Chris, teach them the right way to read a film."

The senior resident didn't show any emotion as he rattled off that the xray was an anterior-posterior view and slightly rotated. The patient appeared to be leaning. It was adequately exposed, the central venous line was in place, and the patient had a nasogastric tube situated in his stomach. There was evidence of bilateral interstitial densities, with a small left pleural effusion. The most likely diagnosis was congestive heart failure.

Dr. Charest was notorious for his rigid teaching style. There was only one correct way of doing any particular task, and it was the way he did it. He took shots at the other interns as well. One was asked to tie her 'unruly' hair. The other, when he failed to give the correct answer to a question, was asked if he thought patients should be paying $5000 a day to stay in an ICU when the responsible doctor wasn't knowledgeable.

Rounds drew to a close an hour later, and visions of my bed began dancing in front of my eyes. I visited all the patients again before leaving, double and triple checking my own list to make sure that I hadn't neglected ordering any medications. I drove myself home 28 hours after the shift had started. The only thought on my mind as I drifted off to sleep minutes after reaching home was that the absentee intern owed me. Big.

Final Thoughts

The residency years allow the fresh graduate to put their learning and skills into action. The pace is fast, the expectations are high. You will be surprised at how fast you gain the ability to confidently assess patients, and start them towards recovery. You will learn to appreciate your own technical proficiency as you place large venous lines directly above patients' hearts; you will feel surprised when you find yourself calmly giving orders in life and death code situations. In the midst of the heavy responsibilities, long hours, poor diet, and minimal personal time, remember your purpose for entering medicine. Use that passion to guide you in your journey towards becoming a skilled and compassionate physician.

Chapter 14: Choosing the Right Specialty

"I think and think for months, for years. Ninety-nine times the conclusion is false. The hundredth time I am right."
- Albert Einstein

Medical school will make you into a doctor, but it won't instruct you on the realities of professional life. What issues are important to the working physician? What factors should you consider when choosing a specialty? This chapter provides the answers to questions about the specialties in demand today, and geographical areas of need. It gives information on the different medical specialties, namely the work environment, training requirements, and physician compensation.

Specialties in Need

There has been a marked shift in the perception of doctor supply in the U.S. since 2003. Over the past three decades, workforce analysts had repeatedly predicted an oversupply of physicians by the year 2000, despite the realization that the American population was expanding and aging. Additionally, the present generation of physicians is putting in less hours as they opt towards more balanced family and work lives, and earlier retirement. Medical organizations had taken heed of the forecasts of a gross physician excess and worked towards curtailing the number of residency positions. With a reduction in the number of specialty graduate positions underway, it then came as a surprise when the Council on

Graduate Medical Education, a federal advisory board, announced an impending physician shortage in late 2003.

There is a lack of specific data on the magnitude of upcoming physician supply, demand and distribution within the country. Whether the real issue is shortages in specific specialties in select areas rather than a nationwide shortage of doctors remains to be seen. The mid-1990's had seen a drive towards encouraging more doctors to enter primary care rather than the specialty fields, with the resulting present shortage in areas such as Radiology and Anesthesiology.

Different specialty groups have been cautioning a decreased supply in the number of physicians based on the residency spots being filled each year. A decline in the number of residents choosing Cardiothoracic Surgery is causing concerns about the ability to accommodate the demand for heart surgeries. A significant percentage of practicing heart surgeons are expected to retire by the end of the decade, adding to the shortage. Cardiologists worry about the insufficient number of post-graduate programs to fill the demand for their specialty over the next twenty years also. Similarly, there has been a declining number of students applying for Neurosurgery and Surgery, for reasons such as heavy workload, long years of training, and lack of personal and family time. These tend to be highly litigious fields, adding to the growing disinterest by U.S. medical students.

A growing shortage of specialists is presently being seen, and is predicted to worsen, among Anesthesiologists, Gerontologists, Cardiologists, Pulmonologists, Urologists, Oncologists, Gastroenterologists, Hematologists and Intensive Care physicians.

A study on the issue of physician shortage was published in the *Journal of the American Medical Association* in December, 2003. The study was conducted by Dr. Richard Cooper and Sandra Stoflet, of the Medical College of Wisconsin, and Dr. Steven Wartman, Dean of the School of Medicine at The University of Texas Health Science Center at San Antonio. Their findings were based on the responses of 58% of the country's medical schools and 86% of state medical societies.

They reported that 85% of polled medical school deans and medical societies felt shortages existed in at least one specialty, with many identifying shortages in multiple specialties. Anesthesiology and Radiology were considered to be the areas with greatest need, followed by Cardiology, Gastroenterology, Geriatrics, Dermatology, Psychiatry, Emergency Medicine and Pediatric subspecialties. General Surgery and surgical subspecialties were also perceived as areas of shortage. 30% of Deans participating in the study felt that there was an under-supply in the number of primary care physicians as well. Internal Medicine was reported as facing a 'severe' shortage, and Family Practice as 'medium' or 'mini-mal'.

State medical societies felt that the shortage among specialists was more severe compared to primary care physicians. Many felt that medical subspecialties had the greatest need, followed by surgical subspecialties, followed by General or Trauma Surgery. Medical society respondents and medical school deans both expressed concerns about the distribution of primary care physicians in the country.

Geographical Areas of Need: How MD's can Contribute and Benefit

The U.S. Public Health Service Act has designated specific regions of the country as health professional shortage areas or medically underserved areas. These locations lack primary health care physicians and resources, and may also indicate areas with a high infant mortality rate or poverty level.

Surprisingly, even in a developed nation with one of the highest standards of living in the world, there are specific pockets in the United States that lack adequate medical attention. As many as 50 million people are estimated to live in communities without adequate primary health care. The extent of physician shortage varies from state to state, and among rural and metropolitan areas. Rural and inner city areas are often the hardest hit, and have experienced shortages in primary medical care for many decades. The fields of Family Practice, General Internal Medicine, Pediatrics and Obstetrics/Gynecology are areas of need for such locations. Underserved areas range from locales within Honolulu, Hawaii to Kings County, New York. For a list of geographical areas of need, visit http://bphc.hrsa.gov/database.htm

In an attempt to distribute health care resources fairly, the United States Department of Health and Human Services funds a program known as the National Health Service Corps (NHSC). Their goal is to attract physicians to underserved regions by providing incentives such as a Loan Repayment Program. In return for a contract for a specified period of fulltime work, such as two years, the NHSC offers a competitive salary, funds for repayment of existing educational loans, and tax relief in addition to the opportunity of making a significant difference in an American community. The Loan Repayment Program is aimed at primary care physicians. Currently, the maximum repayment amount is set at $25,000 per year during an initial two year contract. The contract can be continued on a yearly basis beyond the first two years at a repayment rate of $35,000 per year, as long as educational loans remain. Since underserved areas are available in all states, clinicians have a range of options when choosing a work location.

For more information on job opportunities with the NHSC, contact the NHSC Loan Repayment Program at 1-800-221-9393 or visit http://nhsc.bhpr.hrsa.gov/jobs.

Choosing a Specialty

Most medical school candidates give only a fleeting thought to the specialty that they will pursue after medical school. Prior to medical school, they are limited by their knowledge of the different fields. It is surprising that even medical school does not prepare the student well for choosing a lifelong specialty. The reason is that clinical experience is limited to a few core rotations and electives, and students do not get an opportunity to learn fully about the other possible medical careers, such as Nuclear Medicine and Radiation Oncology. It is even more pronounced in less clinical fields, such as Environmental Medicine, Occupational Medicine, and Pathology.

The trend nowadays is for medical schools to direct students towards earlier decision-making for specialty choices. Students are required to submit applications for residency positions early in the fourth year of medical school. By this time, they will have completed their main rotations in Emergency Medicine, General Surgery, Internal Medicine, Obstetrics and Gynecology and Pediatrics, but electives are often left till the final year of medical school. Electives are rotations that students can use to explore areas of interest. For example, a student who is thinking about becoming a Plastic Surgeon would choose electives in Plastic Surgery. However, by being asked to make earlier decisions, students are picking careers without adequate exposure to the fields.

The reality is that few students are definite about their specialty choice in the first three years of medical school. They may have some idea of the general field that interests them, such as a medical versus surgical specialty, or general practice versus a highly specialized field. Many students end up making decisions only days or even hours prior to the residency application deadlines, without putting much thought beyond their own limited experiences of the field into their decision.

A good method of picking a specialty that allows for a fully informed decision is yet to evolve in medical school curriculums. The time-constrained lecture and clinical rotation schedules do not leave much time for medical schools to inform students about all the different areas, or to provide a better look at each of the specialties. As a result, students are left to their own devices to gather this necessary information. Books such as *How to Choose a Medical Specialty* and Iserson's *Getting into a Residency: A Guide for Medical Students* help to direct students to consider their own motivations and strengths when picking a specialty, and provide valuable information on residency programs.

Factors to Consider When Choosing a Medical Specialty:
- Patient population - do you prefer working with children, adult or geriatric patients, or is a field with technology better suited to your interests (found in specialties like Radiology and Nuclear Medicine)?
- Types of problems: do you prefer working with medical or surgical conditions?
- How important is the use of technology and procedures in your daily work?
- Do you prefer general practice or a highly specialized field?
- Consider lifestyle factors: flexibility, call schedule, hours worked, stress level, compensation
- Do you prefer working in a hospital, clinic or a combination of the two?
- Length of residency training - general practice fields like Family Practice, Internal Medicine and Pediatrics require a shorter period of training
- Geographical location - job opportunities for highly specialized fields are more likely to be found in urban areas that are closer to academic centers
- Increasing areas of need

It is important to start thinking about a specialty as early as the first and second year of medical school. This allows opportunities to get involved in research or part-time work to gain a competitive edge for sought after residency spots in fields such as Dermatology and Plastic Surgery.

The following section highlights the major fields of medicine, training requirements, and areas of subspecialty. Median physician compensation is also provided. It reflects the base annual salary of licensed physicians. It does not include bonuses or benefits. For example, the base salary of an Anesthesiologist is $286,409. With bonuses, the median salary becomes $292,635. If benefits such as 401k/403b plans, healthcare benefits, vacation time, social security, disability and pension are added to this figure, the salary rises to $360,875. These figures were obtained through extensive surveys done by salary.com, and are specific for New York City. More information on different areas of the country can be obtained by visiting salary.com.

Resident salaries are significantly less and, depending on the geographic location, tend to start around $32,000. Each year of training provides an increase in wages, and Chief Residents and Fellows earn approximately $50,000, and above. Information on resident salaries can be obtained from the Fellowship and Residency Electronic Interactive Database (FREIDA) at http://www.ama-assn.org/go/freida.

The Different Fields of Medicine

Anesthesiology
Anesthesiologists are trained in the administration of medications to control pain and level of consciousness. This is particularly necessary during surgeries. They are also experts in cardiopulmonary resuscitation and procedures such as intubation, where a plastic tube is inserted into the airway to allow a sedated or comatose patient to breath.
Types of conditions dealt with: Acute, chronic and cancer pain syndromes, surgical anesthesia, difficult airway management, administering epidurals during childbirth
Years of residency following medical school: 1 year of internship followed by 3 years of Anesthesiology training.
Areas of Subspecialty: Pain Medicine, Critical Care Medicine and Pediatric Anesthesiology; requires 1 additional year of training.
Work Environment: Operating rooms, clinics. Anesthesiologists usually work shifts. On-call responsibilities within the hospital at night is usually confined to emergency surgeries or responding to a 'code', where a patient's heart has stopped beating or the patient is unable to breathe. The Anesthesiologist can help stabilize the patient's breathing by inserting a tube into the trachea, and can also direct other doctors and nurses on the procedures of a code.
Median Physician Compensation: $286,409

Dermatology
Dermatologists diagnose and treat diseases of the skin.
Types of diseases dealt with: Eczema, acne, psoriasis
Years of residency following medical school: 1 year of internship followed by 3 years of Dermatology training
Areas of Subspecialty: Dermatopathology, Clinical and Laboratory Dermatological Immunology, and Pediatric Dermatology; requires 1 additional year of training

Work Environment: Clinics. Hospital and on-call responsibilities are minimal. Dermatology residents carry beepers at home on their days on-call in case they are consulted for an emergency case, but these are rare.
Median Physician Compensation: $213,664

Emergency Medicine
Doctors in Emergency Medicine are trained in diagnosing and managing all acute injuries, life-threatening illnesses, medical and psychiatric diseases. Patients are either treated and discharged from the Emergency Room, or admitted to the hospital under the care of another doctor.
Years of residency following medical school: 3 years of Emergency Medicine training
Types of conditions dealt with: Motor vehicle trauma victims, heart attacks, poisonings, broken bones
Areas of Subspecialty: Medical Toxicology, Pediatric Emergency Medicine: require 2 additional years of training. Sports Medicine: requires 1 additional year of training.
Work Environment: Hospital Emergency Rooms; work shifts; no on-call responsibilities. For rural communities, the number of emergency physicians may be few, so the E.R. may be staffed by family doctors, or an Emergency Room Physician may have on-call responsibilities from home in the nights.
Median Physician Compensation: $225,909

Family Practice
Family doctors provide broad-based medical care in many disciplines for the family unit. Family doctors provide care for children as well as pregnant patients. During residency, Family doctors rotate through the different fields of Pediatrics, Obstetrics, Gynecology, Internal Medicine, Intensive Care, and Emergency Medicine to develop a range of skills. They refer patients to specialists for complicated cases.
Years of residency following medical school: 3 years of Family Practice training
Types of conditions dealt with: Infections, care of chronic diseases such as diabetes, asthma, high blood pressure, cancer.
Areas of Subspecialty: Geriatric Medicine and Sports Medicine: require 1 additional year of training
Work Environment: Clinic and hospital duties; on-call responsibilities for patients on nights and weekends.
Median Physician Compensation: $159,381

Internal Medicine

General Internal Medicine doctors provide broad-based medical care to adults only. A large portion of their practice involves geriatric (older) patients with multiple medical problems. Internal Medicine provides many opportunities for fellowships, from Cardiology to Critical Care Medicine. Residents in a General Internal Medicine program rotate through the Emergency Room, Intensive Care Unit, outpatient clinics and hospital wards.

Years of residency following medical school: 3 years of Internal Medicine training

Types of conditions dealt with: Heart attacks, strokes, pneumonia

Areas of Subspecialty:

Geriatric Medicine, Sports Medicine: require 1 additional year of training

Critical Care Medicine, Endocrinology, Hematology, Infectious Diseases, Medical Oncology, Nephrology, Pulmonary Disease, Rheumatology, Allergy and Immunology: require 2 additional years of training

Cardiology, Gastroenterology, Hematology/Oncology, Pulmonary/Critical Care Medicine: require 3 additional years of training

Clinical Cardiac Electrophysiology, Interventional Cardiology: require 4 additional years of training

Work Environment: Clinics, Hospitals, On-call responsibilities on nights and weekends

Median Physician Compensation:

    General Internal Medicine: $159,976
    Critical Care Medicine: $220,860
    Endocrinologist: $171,774
    Geriatrics: $159,381
    Gastroenterologist: $241,538
    Infectious Diseases: $166,210
    Hematologist/Oncologist: $249,715
    Pulmonary Medicine: $206,485
    Nephrologist: $201,876
    Rheumatologist: $173,063

Medical Genetics

The study of diseases with a genetic basis. Geneticists diagnose, manage and offer information and counseling to parents and patients.

Types of conditions dealt with: Down Syndrome, Neural tube defects

Years of residency following medical school: 4 years, or 2 years of Medical Genetics training in combination with another residency.

Areas of Subspecialty: Molecular Genetic Pathology: requires 1 additional year of training
Work Environment: Clinics, labs, hospital. Geneticists generally work office hours, and there are minimal on-call responsibilities.
Median Physician Compensation: Not available

Neurological Surgery
Neurosurgeons treat disorders and diseases of the nervous system and the brain through surgery.
Years of residency following medical school: 1 year of a General Surgery internship followed by 5 years of Neurological Surgery training
Types of conditions dealt with: Brain tumors or bleeds, spinal cord injuries
Areas of Subspecialty: Endovascular Surgical Neuroradiology: requires 1 additional year of training
Work Environment: Operating rooms, clinics, on-call responsibilities on nights and weekends. A Neurosurgery residency is considered one of the most challenging surgical fields, in terms of extensive on-call responsibilities and complicated nature of performing surgery on the brain and spinal cord.
Median Physician Compensation for Surgeons: $249,309 (Specialized fields such as Neurological Surgery have significantly higher salaries)

Neurology
Neurologists deal with the diagnosis and medical treatment of diseases of the nervous system and the brain.
Years of residency following medical school: 1 year of internship followed by 3 years of Neurology training
Types of conditions dealt with: Seizures, strokes, multiple sclerosis, Parkinson's disease
Areas of Subspecialty: Clinical Neurophysiology, Pain Management, Vascular Neurology: require 1 additional year of training
Work Environment: Clinics, hospital, night and weekend on-call responsibilities
Median Physician Compensation: $181,502

Nuclear Medicine
Nuclear medicine doctors use radioactive and stable nuclide substances to image, diagnose and treat specific conditions
Years of residency following medical school: 1 year of internship followed by 2 years of Nuclear Medicine training
Types of conditions dealt with: Cancers, thyroid disorders, detecting the cause of

bone pain
Work Environment: Hospital, labs. Patient care is limited to managing the patient while obtaining images of the body and organs.
Median Physician Compensation: Not available

Obstetrics and Gynecology

Obstetricians and gynecologists are trained in the care of women, from health maintenance and disease prevention, to pregnancy and birth. They diagnose and treat diseases of the genital and reproductive tracts of women, such as the uterus and ovaries. They are trained to perform surgeries such as hysterectomies (removal of the uterus and/or ovaries) and cesarean sections.
Years of residency following medical school: 4 years of obstetrics/gynecological training
Types of conditions dealt with: Ovarian tumors, miscarriages, osteoporosis
Work Environment: Clinics and hospital; night and weekend on-call responsibilities. Doctors practicing obstetrics often have extensive night call responsibilities due to the nature of babies arriving at all hours of the day.
Median Physician Compensation: $225,218

Ophthalmology

Ophthalmologists are trained in the medical and surgical diagnosis and management of eye disorders.
Years of residency following medical school: 1 year of internship followed by 3 years of ophthalmology training
Types of conditions dealt with: cataracts, glaucoma, near and far sightedness
Work Environment: Clinics, hospital; minimal on-call responsibility. Residents tend to carry beepers from home in case of emergency consultations.
Median Physician Compensation: $216,543

Orthopedic Surgery

Orthopedic surgeons are trained to perform surgery for diseases of the bone, joints and ligaments. They also diagnose and direct the medical and physical management of musculoskeletal disorders.
Years of residency following medical school: 5 years of orthopedic training
Types of conditions dealt with: Bone fractures, bone tumors
Areas of Subspecialty: Adult Reconstructive Surgery, Foot & Ankle Surgery, Hand Surgery, Musculoskeletal Oncology, Pediatric Spinal Surgery, Sports Medicine, Trauma Medicine; require 1 additional year of training
Work Environment: Operating rooms, hospital wards, clinics; night and week-

end on-call responsibilities.
Median Physician Compensation: $339,886

Otolaryngology

Otolaryngologists deal with the diagnosis and medical and surgical treatment of disorders of the ears, nose and throat, including Head and Neck Surgery
Years of residency following medical school: 1 year of a General Surgery internship followed by 4 years of Otolaryngology training
Types of conditions dealt with: Nasal septum surgeries, ear injuries, nasal cancers
Areas of Subspecialty: Nerutology and Pediatric Otolaryngology; requires 2 additional years of training
Work Environment: Clinics, operating rooms; night and weekend on-call responsibilities.
Median Physician Compensation: $289,052

Pathology-Anatomic and Clinical

A Pathologist diagnoses diseases by studying cells and tissues microscopically.
Years of residency following medical school: 4 years of Pathology training
Types of conditions dealt with: diagnosing blood cancers, blood clotting disorders
Areas of Subspecialty: Blood Banking, Chemical Pathology, Cytopathology Dermatopathology, Forensic Pathology, Hematology, Medical Microbiology, Molecular Genetic Pathology and Pediatric Pathology require 1 additional year of training. Neuropathology requires 2 additional years of training.
Work Environment: Hospital labs; minimal night and weekend on-call responsibilities. Limited direct patient care.
Median Physician Compensation: $220,211

Pediatrics

Pediatricians care for children from birth through adolescence by diagnosing and managing developmental disorders and medical diseases.
Years of residency following medical school: 3 years of Pediatrics training
Types of conditions dealt with: Childhood vaccinations, infections, growth disorders
Areas of Subspecialty: Sports Medicine requires 1 additional year of training. Adolescent Medicine, Critical Care Medicine, Endocrinology, Hematology/Oncology, Neonatal/Perinatal Medicine, Nephrology and Pulmonology require 2 additional years of training.

Cardiology, Developmental-Behavioral Medicine, Emergency Medicine, Gastroenterology, Infectious Disease and Rheumatology require 3 additional years of training.

Work Environment: Clinics and hospital; night and weekend on-call responsibilities

Median Physician Compensation: $151,104

Physical Medicine and Rehabilitation

Physiatrists improve the physical function of patients disabled from disease or injury.

Years of residency following medical school: 1 year of internship followed by 3 years of Physical Medicine and Rehabilitation training

Types of conditions dealt with: Stroke rehabilitation, traumatic brain injuries

Areas of Subspecialty: Pain Medicine and Spinal Cord Injury Medicine: require 1 additional year of training. Pediatric Rehabilitation: requires 2 additional years of training.

Work Environment: Clinics and hospital; minimal night and weekend on-call responsibilities

Median Physician Compensation: $202,409

Plastic Surgery

Plastic Surgeons aim to reconstruct body function or appearance through surgery

Years of residency following medical school: 3 years of a General Surgery program followed by 2-3 years of Plastic Surgery training; or a 5-6 year combined program. Residents who have completed an Orthopedic Surgery, Urology, Neurosurgery or Otolaryngology program are also eligible to pursue Plastic Surgery in a 2-3 year program.

Types of conditions dealt with: Facial reconstruction after tumor removal, burns, cosmetic surgery

Areas of Subspecialty: Craniofacial surgery and Hand Surgery: require 1 additional year of training

Work Environment: Clinics, operating room, hospital wards; night and weekend on-call responsibilities

Median Physician Compensation for all surgeons: $249,309 (Plastic surgery is one of the highest paying surgical fields, and the quoted figure is an underestimation of a Plastic Surgeon's earning capacity)

Preventive Medicine

Doctors in Preventive Medicine practice in Public Health Medicine, Occupational

Medicine and Aerospace Medicine. Their goal is the prevention of disease and disability.
Years of residency following medical school: 2 to 3 years
Types of conditions dealt with: Environmental exposures in the workplace, health of crew and passengers of air and space transportation
Areas of Subspecialty: Undersea and Hyperbaric Medicine: requires 1 additional year of training. Toxicology: requires 2 additional years of training
Work Environment: Office; work sites
Median Physician Compensation (for Occupational Medicine): $168,752

Psychiatry
Psychiatrists diagnose and treat mental illnesses.
Years of residency following medical school: 4 years of Psychiatric training
Types of conditions dealt with: Depression, schizophrenia, suicide attempts
Areas of Subspecialty: Addiction Psychiatry, Forensic Psychiatry, Geriatric Psychiatry, Pain Management and Psychosomatic Medicine: require 1 additional year of training. Child and Adolescent Psychiatry: requires 2 years of additional training
Work Environment: Clinics, hospitals; night and weekend on-call responsibilities
Median Physician Compensation: $171,163

Radiation Oncology
Radiation Oncologists treat tumors and cancers with ionizing radiation.
Years of residency following medical school: 1 year of internship followed by 4 years of Radiation Oncology training
Types of conditions dealt with: Lung cancer, prostate cancer, breast cancer
Work Environment: Clinics; minimal night and weekend on-call responsibilities
Median Physician Compensation: Not available

Radiology-Diagnostic
Diagnostic Radiologists use radiant energy to diagnose medical and surgical conditions. They interpret images obtained through X-rays, CT scans, MRI's, PET scans, ultrasound machines and nuclear medicine.
Years of residency following medical school: 1 year of internship followed by 4 years of Diagnostic Radiology training
Types of conditions dealt with: Diagnosis of pneumonias, strokes, obstruction in the intestines
Areas of Subspecialty: Abdominal, Cardiothoracic, Endovascular Surgical

Neuroradiology, Musculoskeletal, Neuroradiology, Nuclear Radiology, Pediatrics and Vascular/Interventional Radiology require 1 additional year of training.
Work Environment: Clinics and hospital; minimal night and weekend on-call responsibilities. Most Radiologists work shifts.
Median Physician Compensation: $297,181

Surgery-General
A General Surgeon treats diseases of the stomach, small and large intestines, gall-bladder, adrenal glands, liver, appendix and pancreas surgically.
Years of residency following medical school: 5 years of General Surgery training
Types of conditions dealt with: Abdominal tumors, hernias, appendicitis
Areas of Subspecialty: Critical Care Surgery, Hand Surgery, Colon and Rectal Surgery, and Vascular Surgery: require 1 additional year of training. Thoracic Surgery and Pediatric Surgery: require 2 additional years of training
Work Environment: Operating room, clinics, hospital wards; night and weekend on-call responsibilities
Median Physician Compensation: $249,309

Urology
Urologists diagnose and treat disorders of the urinary and genital tract medically and surgically.
Years of residency following medical school: 1 year of General Surgery internship followed by 4 years of Urology training, or 2 years of General Surgery and 3 years of Urology training
Types of conditions dealt with: Enlarged prostate, bladder cancer
Areas of Subspecialty: Pediatric Urology requires 1 additional year of training
Work Environment: Clinics, operating rooms, hospital wards; night and weekend on-call responsibilities
Median Physician Compensation: $258,691

Conclusion:

"Nothing happens until something moves."
- Albert Einstein

If your intention when you picked up this book was to find out what it takes to become a doctor, I hope you've come away with the knowledge of not only how to get into medical school, but what it means to train as a doctor. Practicing medicine is a challenge, but no more than any other profession if your heart is in it. Discover this aspect about yourself first, as it is the most important. And once you have decided that it is the right path for you, pursue it with single-minded determination.

By now, you have learnt what it takes to get into medical school. Whether you are currently a high school or college student, or a non-traditional candidate, becoming aware of your various options is the first step to realizing your dreams. Allopathic or osteopathic, American education or a foreign medical degree - consider them all.

Medicine isn't a field which you will be able to disengage from at the end of the day. Choose it only if you are willing to give all your energy and time to it, at least during the training years. As you speak to doctors, you will find that even those who have been practicing for over forty years continue to do so with an all-consuming dedication and passion. There aren't many careers left that are lifelong, but medicine continues to be one of them. Talk to as many doctors as you can, and weigh their opinions carefully. Balance the positives against the negatives, and ultimately, make the decision that is right for you. Happy Journey.

Appendix A

The following schools offer combined Bachelor of Science/Doctor of Medicine and/or Bachelor of Arts/Doctor of Medicine degrees for high school students. Contact each one directly for admissions information.

MEDICAL COLLEGES	WEBSITES
Albany Medical College (New York)	http://www.amc.edu/academic/college
Boston University School of Medicine	http://www.bumc.bu.edu
Brown Medical School (Rhode Island)	http://bms.brown.edu/admissions
Chicago Medical School	http://www.finchcms.edu/cms
David Geffen School of Medicine at UCLA	http://www.biomed.ucr.edu/bsmd/index.html
Drexel University College of Medicine (Pennsylvania)	http://www.drexel.edu/med
East Tennessee State University	http://com.etsu.edu
George Washington University School of Medicine and Health Sciences (District of Columbia)	http://www.gwumc.edu/smhs
Jefferson Medical College of Thomas Jefferson University (Pennsylvania)	http://www.jefferson.edu/main
Keck School of Medicine of the University of Southern California	http://college.usc.edu/bamd

MEDICAL COLLEGES	WEBSITES
Meharry Medical College School of Medicine (Tennessee)	http://www.mmc.edu/medschool
Michigan State University College of Human Medicine	http://www.chm.msu.edu/chmhome/admissions/medschol.htm
New Jersey Medical School, University of Medicine and Dentistry of New Jersey	http://njms.umdnj.edu
Northeastern Ohio Universities College of Medicine	http://www.neoucom.edu
Feinberg School of Medicine, Northwestern University (Illinois)	http://www.feinberg.northwestern.edu/hpme
Ohio State University College of Medicine and Public Health	http://medicine.osu.edu/futurestudents/eap.cfm
Robert Wood Johnson Medical School, University of Medicine and Dentistry of New Jersey	http://rwjms.umdnj.edu

Sophie Davis School o Biomedical Education/City College of New York	fhttp://med.cuny.edu
St. Lewis University School of Medicine (Missouri)	http://medschool.slu.edu
State University of New York Downstate Medical Center College of Medicine	http://sls.downstate.edu/admissions
State University of New York Upstate Medical University College of Medicine	http://www.upstate.edu/com
Stony Brook University Health Sciences Center School of Medicine (New York)	http://www.hsc.stonybrook.edu/som
Temple University School of Medicine (Pennsylvania)	http://www.medschool.temple.edu
The Texas A & M University System Health Science Center College of Medicine	http://tamushsc.tamu.edu
Tufts University School of Medicine (Massachusetts)	http://www.tufts.edu/med
University of Alabama School of Medicine	http://main.uab.edu/uasom
University of California, San Diego School of Medicine	http://medicine.ucsd.edu

MEDICAL COLLEGES	**WEBSITES**
University of Cincinnati College of Medicine	http://www.med.uc.edu
University of Connecticut School of Medicine	http://medicine.uchc.edu
University of Florida College of Medicine	http://www.med.ufl.edu
University of Miami School of Medicine	http://www.med.miami.edu
University of Missouri-Columbia School of Medicine	http://www.muhealth.org/~medicine
University of Missouri-Kansas City School of Medicine	http://research.med.umkc.edu
University of Rochester School of Medicine and Dentistry (New York)	http://www.urmc.rochester.edu/smd
University of South Alabama College of Medicine	http://www.southalabama.edu/com
University of South Florida College of Medicine	http://hsc.usf.edu/medicine
University of Wisconsin Medical School	http://www.med.wisc.edu
Virginia Commonwealth University School of Medicine	http://www.medschool.vcu.edu

Appendix B

List of Foreign Medical Schools

The following foreign medical school programs have been popular choices for American and Canadian students. With the exception of the Universidad Autonoma De Guadalajara, the schools listed offer their curriculum in English. The inclusion of schools in the list below does not imply recommendation for any particular institution. Students are advised to research each school thoroughly using the criteria outlined in Chapter 9. Pay attention to the political stability of the country to ensure personal safety. European schools that accept foreign medical students, but do not offer a solely English curriculum have not been included. For further information on these schools, consult the World Directory of Medical Schools at http://www.who.int.

AUSTRALIA

Medical School	Length of training (years)	Year established	International Quota (# of seats)
School of Medicine The Flinders University of South Australia Flinders Drive PO Box 2100 Adelaide 5001 South Australia Tel.: +61 (8) 820 441 60 http://www.flinders.edu.au/	4	1975	30-32
School of Medicine The University Of Queensland Herston Road Herston 4006 Queensland Australia Tel.: +61 (7) 336 552 78 http://www.som.uq.edu.au/som/home.shtml	4	1936	20
Faculty Of Medicine University Of Melbourne Grattan Street Parkville 3050 Victoria Australia Tel.: +61 (3) 934 458 90 http://www.unimelb.edu.au	6	1862	75 for a combined undergraduate and medical degree; 10 for medical degree only

Medical School	Length of training (years)	Year established	International Quota (# of seats)
Faculty Of Medicine And Dentistry University Of Western Australia Mounts Bay Road, Nedlands Perth 6907 Western Australia Tel.: +61 (8) 934 623 16 http://www.uwa.edu.au/	6	1957	15
Faculty Of Medicine University Of New South Wales Anzac Parade Sydney 2052 New South Wales Australia Tel.: +61 (2) 938 524 54 http://www.med.unsw.edu.au	6	1961	40
Faculty Of Medicine University Of Sydney Sydney 2006 New South Wales Australia Tel.: +61 (2) 935 131 32 http://www.medfac.usyd.edu.au/	4	1883	60

DOMINICA

School of Medicine Ross University PO Box 266 Roseau Dominica Tel.:1 732 978-5300 (NJ) http://www.rossmed.edu/	5	1978	Student body comprised of international students

Medical School	Length of training (years)	Year established	International Quota (# of seats)
GRENADA			
St George's University School Of Medicine University Centre Po Box 7 St George's Grenada Tel.: 1473 444 4357 http://www.stgeorgesuniv.edu/	4	1977	Student body comprised of international students
INDIA			
Kasturba Medical College Manipal Academy Of Higher Education Light House Hill Road Po Box 53 Mangalore 575001 Tel.: +91 (824) 423 452/423 654/426 482 http://www.manipal.edu/kmc/index.htm	5 years plus one year of internship	1955	25%
Kasturba Medical College Manipal Academy Of Higher Education Po Box 8 Manipal 576119 Tel.: +91 (8252) 712 01 http://www.manipal.edu/kmc/index.htm	5 years plus one year of internship	1953	25%
Medical College Bombay University Pune-Mumbai highway Kamothe New Bombay 410209 Tel.: +91 (22) 742 1723 http://www.mgmmumbai.com/	5 years	1989	15

Medical School	Length of training (years)	Year established	International Quota (# of seats)
IRELAND			
Medical School Royal College Of Surgeons In Ireland 123 St Stephen's Green Dublin Tel.: +353 (1) 402 2281 http://www.rcsi.ie/	5-6 plus 1 year of internship	1784	Not available
Faculty Of Health Sciences University Of Dublin Trinity College Dublin, Ireland Tel.: +353 (1) 608 1000 http://www.tcd.ie/	5 plus 1 year of internship	1711	Not available
ISRAEL			
Sackler School of Medicine Tel Aviv University Ramat Aviv Tel Aviv-Yafo 69978 Israel Tel: (212) 688-8811 (NY) http://www.tau.ac.il/medicine/ Offers New York State-	4	1964	300 American students in 4 year MD program

American Program, established 1976.

MEXICO

Medical School	Length of training (years)	Year established	International Quota (# of seats)
Facultad De Medicina	5-6	1935	Admits significant number of North American students

Universidad Autonoma De Guadalajara
Avenida Patria 1201
Lomas Del Valle 3A
Apdo 1-440
Guadalajara
Mexico
Tel.: +52 (3) 641 7051/641 5051

http://www.uag.mx/medicine/

Medical School	Length of training (years)	Year established	International Quota (# of seats)
NETHERLANDS ANTILLES			
Saba School of Medicine PO Box 1000 Saba Netherlands Antilles Tel.: +599 (4) 634 56 http://www.saba.edu/	4	1993	Student body comprised of international students
NEW ZEALAND			
Otago Medical School University Of Otago Great King Street Po Box 913 Dunedin Tel.: +64 (3) 479 5057 http://osms.otago.ac.nz/main/	6	1875	Not available
NORTHERN IRELAND			
College Of Medicine And Health Sciences The Queen's University Of Belfast 71 University Road Belfast BT7 1NF Tel.: +44 (1232) 245 133 http://www.qub.ac.uk/	5	1849	Not available
SCOTLAND			
Faculty Of Medicine And Medical Sciences University Of Aberdeen Polwarth Building Foresterhill Aberdeen AB9 2ZD Tel.: +44 (1224) 681 818 http://www.abdn.ac.uk/sras/	5	1497	13

Medical School	Length of training (years)	Year established	International Quota (# of seats)
Medical School University Of Edinburgh Teviot Place Edinburgh EH8 9AG http://www.ed.ac.uk/	5	1728	16
Faculty of Medicine Wolfson Medical School Building University Avenue University of Glasgow G12 8QQ Tel: 0141 330 6216 http://www.gla.ac.uk/	5	1637	17

UNITED KINGDOM 0F GREAT BRITAIN AND NORTHERN IRELAND

School Of Medicine University Of Leeds Worsley Medical And Dental Building Thoresby Place Leeds LS2 9Nl Tel.: +44 (113) 233 4364 http://www.leeds.ac.uk/	5	1831	15
School Of Medicine University Of Leicester Maurice Shock Medical Sciences Building University Road Po Box 138 Leicester Le1 9Hn Tel.: +44 (116) 252 2966	5	1975	13
King's College School Of Medicine And Dentistry University Of London Bessemer Road London Se5 9Pj Tel.: +44 (171) 312 5622 http://www.kcl.ac.uk/	5	1831	27

Appendix B

Medical School	Length of training (years)	Year established	International Quota (# of seats)
Royal Free Hospital School Of Medicine University Of London Rowland Hill Street London Nw3 2Pf Tel.: +44 (171) 794 0500 http://www.ucl.ac.uk/	5	1874	26
Medical School The University Of Nottingham Queen's Medical Centre Nottingham Ng7 2Uh Tel.: +44 (115) 970 9379	5	1970	25

Appendix C

Canadian Medical Schools
University of Alberta, Faculty of Medicine and Oral Health Sciences

- Location: Edmonton, Alberta
- Year established: 1913
- Language of curriculum: English
- Duration of medical studies: 4 years
- Minimum undergraduate work required: 2 years
- MCAT required: Yes
- Reserved seats: 85% for residents of Alberta, Yukon, Northwest Territories, Nunavut. 15% for out of province students
- Number of students accepted per year: 125
- Accepts international students: No
- Special consideration: Mature applicants; Masters and PhD candidates are given additional points
- Combined programs: MD/PhD

For further information, contact:
Faculty of Medicine and Oral Health Sciences
University of Alberta
2-45 Medical Sciences Building
Edmonton, Alberta T6G 2R7
Tel.: (403) 492 6350
http://www.med.ualberta.ca

University of British Columbia, Faculty of Medicine

- Location: Vancouver, British Columbia
- Year established: 1950
- Language of curriculum: English
- Duration of medical studies: 4 years
- Minimum undergraduate work required: 3 years
- MCAT required: Yes
- Minimum GPA requirement: 2.8/4.0

- Reserved seats: Preference given to residents of B.C, Yukon, Northwest Territories and Nunavut. Limited number of seats for out of province applicants.
- Number of students accepted per year: 200
- Accepts international students: No
- Special consideration: Aboriginal applicants, students from or interested in working in rural communities
- Combined programs: MD/PhD

For further information, contact:
Faculty of Medicine
University of British Columbia
3250-910 West 10TH Avenue
Vancouver, British Columbia V5T 4E3
Tel.: (604) 875 4500
http://www.med.ubc.ca

University of Calgary, Faculty of Medicine

- Location: Calgary, Alberta
- Year established: 1970
- Language of curriculum: English
- Duration of medical studies: 4 years
- Minimum undergraduate work required: 2 years
- MCAT required: Yes
- Minimum MCAT scores: None specified
- Reserved seats: 85% for provincial residents; 15% for out of province students
- Number of students accepted per year: 100
- Accepts international students: Yes, only if partnership exists with foreign government. American students are not eligible.
- Special consideration: Encourages applications from aboriginal population
- Combined programs: MD/MSc, MD/PhD

For further information, contact:
Faculty of Medicine
University of Calgary
Health Sciences Center
3330 Hospital Drive N.W.

Calgary, Alberta T2N 4NI
Tel.: (403) 220 4246
http://www.med.ucalgary.ca/admissions

University of Manitoba, Faculty of Medicine

- Location: Winnipeg, Manitoba
- Year established: 1883
- Language of curriculum: English
- Duration of medical studies: 4 years
- Minimum undergraduate work required: 4 years
- MCAT required: Yes
- Minimum GPA requirement: 3.0/4.0
- Reserved seats: 90% for provincial residents; 10% for out of province residents
- Number of students accepted per year: Approximately 88
- Accepts international students: No
- Special consideration: Manitoba residents with previous experience relevant to medicine; aboriginal populations and applicants sponsored by a Faculty approved agency, such as the Armed Forces. These candidates are subject to different weighting of the admissions criteria.
- Combined Programs: MD/PhD

For further information, contact:
Faculty of Medicine
University of Manitoba
753 McDermot Avenue
Winnipeg, Manitoba R3T 2N2
Tel.: (204) 789 3569
http://www.umanitoba.ca/faculties/medicine

Memorial University of Newfoundland, Faculty of Medicine

- Location: St. John's, Newfoundland
- Year established: 1969
- Language of curriculum: English
- Duration of medical studies: 4 years
- Minimum undergraduate work required: 4 years
- MCAT required: Yes

- Minimum GPA requirement: None specified
- Reserved seats: 67% for Newfoundland and Labrador residents, 16% for New Brunswick residents, 3% for Prince Edward Island residents, 7% other Canadian residents, 7% Non-Canadians
- Number of students accepted per year: 60
- Accepts international students: Yes
- Percentage of international students per class: 7
- Special consideration: There aren't any reserved seats for minority or nontraditional candidates, but the Faculty of Medicine will consider the backgrounds of all applicants
- Combined programs: MD/PhD

For further information, contact:
Faculty of Medicine
Memorial University of Newfoundland
300 Prince Phillip Drive
St. John's, Newfoundland A1B 3V6
Tel.: (709) 737 6602
http://www.med.mun.ca/admissions

Dalhousie University, Faculty of Medicine

- Location: Halifax, Nova Scotia
- Year established: 1868
- Language of curriculum: English
- Duration of medical studies: 4 years
- Minimum undergraduate work required: Bachelor's degree
- MCAT required: Yes
- Reserved seats: 90% for maritime residents; 10% for other Canadians and international applicants
- Number of students accepted per year: 90
- Accepts international students: Yes
- Special consideration: Residents of Nova Scotia, New Brunswick, Prince Edward Island
- Combined Programs: MD/PhD program

For further information, contact:
Faculty of Medicine
Dalhousie University

5849 University Avenue
Halifax, Nova Scotia B2T 1E8
Tel.: (902) 494 6592
http://www.medicine.dal.ca

McMaster University, Faculty of Health Sciences

- Location: Hamilton, Ontario
- Year established: 1969
- Language of curriculum: English
- Duration of medical studies: 3 years
- Minimum undergraduate work required: 3 years
- MCAT required: No
- Minimum GPA requirement: 3.0/4.0
- Accepts international students: Yes; up to 10 positions are available. For the classes of 2004-2006, 1 international applicant was chosen per year.
- Special consideration: Residents of Ontario who are mature applicants, have made exceptional contributions to society, aboriginal applicants.

For further information, contact:
Faculty of Health Sciences
McMaster University
1200 Main Street West
Hamilton, Ontario L8N 3Z5
Tel.: (905) 525 9140
http://www.fhs.mcmaster.ca/mdprog

Queen's University, Faculty of Medicine

- Location: Kingston, Ontario
- Year established: 1854
- Language of curriculum: English
- Duration of medical studies: 4 years
- Minimum undergraduate work required: 3 years
- MCAT required: Yes
- Accepts international students: No, except children of alumni
- Special consideration: Aboriginal applicants
- Combined Programs: MD/PhD

Note: Queen's University does not given preference to provincial residents.
For further information, contact:
Faculty of Medicine
Queen's University
Botterell Hall
Kingston, Ontario K7L 3N6
Tel.: (613) 545 2544
http://meds.queensu.ca/medicine

University of Western Ontario, Faculty of Medicine

- Location: London, Ontario
- Year established: 1882
- Language of curriculum: English
- Duration of medical studies: 4 years
- Minimum undergraduate work required: 3 years
- MCAT required: Yes
- Reserved seats: 3 seats for aboriginal applicants, 3 for MD/PhD candidates
- Number of students accepted per year: 133
- Accepts international students: No
- Special consideration: Residents of 519 area code
- Combined programs: MD/PhD

For further information, contact:
Faculty of Medicine
University of Western Ontario
Health Sciences Center
London, Ontario N6A 5C1
Tel.: (519) 661 3744
http://www.med.uwo.ca

University of Ottawa, Faculty of Health Sciences
- Location: Ottawa, Ontario
" Year established: 1945
- Language of curriculum: English, French
- Duration of medical studies: 4 years
- Minimum undergraduate work required: 3 years
- MCAT required: No
  - Minimum GPA requirement: varies yearly.

- Number of students accepted per year: 123
- Accepts international students: No, except children of alumni from Faculty of Medicine
- Special consideration: Preference given to candidates bilingual in French and English. Aboriginal applicants are encouraged to apply. Francophone minority students in Canada from provinces other than Ontario and Quebec can apply for positions above the quota of 123 students through the "Centre national de formation en santé" program.

For further information, contact:
Faculty of Health Sciences
University of Ottawa
451 Smyth Road
Ottawa, Ontario K1H 8M5
Tel.: (613) 562 5800
http://www.uottawa.ca/academic/med

Northern Ontario Medical School

- Location: Northern communities in Ontario. Main campuses in Thunder Bay and Sudbury.
- Year established: 2005
- Language of curriculum: English
- Duration of medical studies: 4 years
- Minimum undergraduate work required: 4 year undergraduate degree, with an exception for mature students who will be considered with a 3 year undergraduate degree.
- MCAT required: No
- Minimum GPA requirement: To be announced
- Reserved seats: Minimum 2 seats per year for aboriginal students
- Number of students accepted per year: 56
- Accepts international students: No
- Special consideration: Candidates from or interested in working in rural areas, as well as francophone, aboriginal and mature candidates.

For further information, contact:
Office of Associate Dean of Admissions and Student Affairs
Northern Ontario Medical School
West Campus

955 Oliver Road
Thunder Bay ON Canada P7B 5E1
Telephone: (807) 343 8100
http://www.normed.ca

University of Toronto, Faculty of Medicine

- Location: Toronto, Ontario
- Year established: 1887
- Language of curriculum: English
- Duration of medical studies: 4 years
- Minimum undergraduate work required: 3 years
- MCAT required: Yes
- Number of students accepted per year: 198
- Accepts international students: Yes; maximum of 7 spots per year
- Combined Programs: MD/PhD

There is no preference given to residents of the province of Ontario.
For further information, contact:
Faculty of Medicine
University of Toronto
1 King's College Circle
Toronto, Ontario M5S 1A8
Tel.: (416) 978 6585
http://www.library.utoronto.ca/medicine/
student_info/acad_undergrad.html

McGill University, Faculty of Medicine

- Location: Montreal, Quebec
- Year established: 1829
- Language of curriculum: English
- Duration of medical studies: 4 years
- Minimum undergraduate work required: 4 years of undergraduate studies leading to a Bachelors degree
- MCAT required: Yes
- Reserved seats: Up to 22 spots for U.S. and international applicants; 5-7 spots for out of province Canadians
- Number of students accepted per year: 160

- Accepts international students: Yes. Encourages applications from American students.
- Combined Programs: MD-PhD, MD-MBA

For further information, contact:
Faculty of Medicine
McGill University
McIntyre Medical Sciences Building
3655 Drummond Street
Montreal, Quebec H3G 1Y6
Tel.: (514) 398 3515
http://www.med.mcgill.ca/admissions

Université de Montréal, Faculté de Médecine

- Location: Montreal, Quebec
- Year established: 1843
- Language of curriculum: French
- Duration of medical studies: 4 years
- Minimum undergraduate work required: Under Quebec regulations, a diploma of collegial studies and two years of a Health Sciences College Program.
- MCAT required: No
- Number of students accepted per year: Approximately 220-227
- Accepts international students: Yes
- Special consideration: French-speaking candidates from other Canadian provinces and U.S.
- Combined Programs: MD/MSc, MD/PhD

For further information, contact:
Faculté de Médecine
Université de Montréal
CP 6128
Succursale Centre-ville
Montreal, Quebec H3C 3J7
Tel.: (514) 343-6265
http://www.umontreal.ca

Université de Sherbrooke, Faculté de Médecine

- Location: Sherbrooke, Quebec
- Year established: 1966
- Language of curriculum: French
- Duration of medical studies: 4 years
- Minimum undergraduate work required: Under Quebec regulations, 2 years of college or a Bachelors degree.
- MCAT required: No
- Reserved seats: 112 spots for Quebec residents, 15 spots for New Brunswick residents, 1 spot for Prince Edward Island residents, 1 spot for Nova Scotia residents and 2 spots for international applicants.
- Number of students accepted per year: Approximately 130
- Accepts international students: Yes
- Combined Programs: MD/MSc

For further information, contact:
Faculté de Médecine
Université de Sherbrooke
3001 12 Avenue Nord
Fleurimont
Sherbrooke, Quebec J1H 5N4
Tel.: (819) 564 5203
http://www.usherbrooke.ca

University of Saskatchewan, College of Medicine

- Location: Saskatoon, Saskatchewan
- Year established: 1953
- Language of curriculum: English
- Duration of medical studies: 4 years
- Minimum undergraduate work required: 2 years (completed prior to applying)
- MCAT required: Yes
- Reserved seats: Up to 6 spots for out of province students; 3 spots for aboriginal candidates
- Number of students accepted per year: 60
- Accepts international students: No

For further information, contact:
College of Medicine
University of Saskatchewan
107 Wiggins Road
Saskatoon, Saskatchewan S7N 5E5
Tel.: (306) 966 6135
http://www.usask.ca/medicine

Université Laval, Faculté de Médecine

- Location: Ste-Foy, Quebec
- Year established: 1853
- Language of curriculum: French
- Duration of medical studies: 4 years
- Minimum undergraduate work required: Under Quebec regulations, two years of college in a Health Sciences Program and the Diploma of Collegial Studies is required. A Bachelors degree in Biological or Health Sciences is acceptable.
- MCAT required: No
- Number of students accepted per year: 187
- Accepts international students: Yes
- Special consideration: Preference to Quebec residents. Will consider French speaking candidates from other Canadian provinces and the U.S.

For further information, contact:
Université Laval
Faculté de Médecine
Ste-Foy, Quebec G1K 7P4
Tel.: (418) 656-2131